To Vicky & Tony,
a pleasure to know,
with ~~best~~ wishes,
Richard

I Want to
Tell You a Story...

2. 8. 12.
Bideford.

GW00716381

Richard Small

Edward Gaskell
Devon

First published 2012
Edward Gaskell publishers
Park Cottage
East-the-Water
Bideford
Devon
EX39 4AS

ISBN 978-1-906769-35-2

I want to tell you a story. . .

Richard Small

Typeset, printed and bound by
Lazarus Press
Caddsdown Business Park
Bideford
Devon
EX39 3DX
www.lazaruspress.com

Dedicated to the one who really matters. . .
You, the reader.

Edward Gaskell *publishers*
DEVON

About the Author

Richard John Small was born in 1948, at the site of the old Workhouse in the industrial town of Bedford. In later life he discovered it was also the place in which his great, great, grandfather had died a pauper in 1885. Richard grew up in a Victorian terraced house with only a small sunless concrete yard for a garden, a house in which water came from a solitary cold tap and heat from a solitary coal fire. Those were the days in which many of the 1840s street slums were being demolished for future development, and when vegetables, coal and milk were sold door to door from a horse and cart. He attended the same schools as did his grandmother before him, and with the exception of one truly brilliant English teacher, Richard's education was all it needed to be for the factory fodder so many were destined to become. It was an intimidating school, with violence and abuse frequently perpetrated by teachers and pupils alike.

After leaving school, Richard pursued a scientific career until it was clear this vocation would not provide enough money to care for his new wife and child, and so he joined the fire service in the summer of 1974, working long anti-social shifts to make ends meet. He endured fire-fighting during the drought year of 1976 and he was made union branch secretary just before the gruelling ten week Fire Services strike of 1977/78. To better his life style and that of his family he moved Counties to where they lived in a rural community, growing vegetables and keeping chickens in the sort of town where you could still leave your keys in the car while shopping.

Richard has always struggled with issues of self-esteem, and despite his best efforts, suffered a painful divorce and eventual estrangement from his beloved children. He was retired from the Fire Service on mental health grounds after more than 25 years of dedicated service.

Richard says he has been kept 'reasonably sane' by the practice of Aikido (in which he attained 3rd Dan) and his fascination with the spiritual development of the 'Self' through the absorbing art of Tai Chi, in which he has become a well-respected teacher.

Richard began to travel in the later years of his life, and has made numerous trips to both Russia and China. He is also a long term supporter of the environmental group Greenpeace, and has planted a virtual forest of trees wherever he has set up home. He says his personal philosophy 'tends to an ethical view on life'.

On retirement, Richard returned to the land of his ancestors in the South West of England, and it is here where he has been inspired to put pen to paper, writing metaphorically in the blood of his life, and of his own understandings.

'I met him at the crossroads, a man with but a cloak and staff. . .'
'. . .we all sat together at the board and we were happy with the man for there was a silence and a mystery in him. . .'
'He told us many a tale that night and also the next day, but what I now record was born out of the bitterness of his days though he himself was kindly, and these tales are of the dust and patience of his road.'
From 'The Wanderer'
by Kahlil Gibran

We cannot fail to be coloured by the dust of our road, can we?

'This book is also for my parents, who will sadly never get to read it, nor ever know it was written, and yet without whom it couldn't have existed. And also for my dear grandchildren Jocey and Sam, who before they were even born were the continuing inspiration and purpose for all I have done, and who I hope, one day, will come to know me the better because of it.

They are the hope for the future, and the guardians of the past.

I in turn thank my ancestors for the journey they made that carried me here today.'

'Du re bo genen ni oll'

You may contact the author via:
www.goodshortstories.weebly.com
www.taichidevon.weebly.com

Contents

Philosophical

A Tale of Two Otters.

Bright young grass gleamed a vibrant green in the warm late spring sunshine, and small birds happily sang their little hearts out from the safety of a clump of great and ancient Yews that stood sentinel in that special place. Apart from the bird song and the soft and almost reverent crunch of shoes on gravel, for a town, it was remarkably peaceful here.

So reminiscent of those childhood days long gone when children could ride their bicycles unfettered along miles of country lanes, their only care to make sure they were back in time for tea, when coal was delivered by horse and cart, when summers were hot and winters were cold; He smiled and felt the feelings of those childhood days.

His closest friend, his old childhood pal, Bob, had lived a few doors away from him in a small rented cottage on the edge of the village, backed on to by a wild wood banked and crystal stream and only shouting distance from their favourite 'conker' tree on the small and ancient village green; the place of so many happy hours.

He himself had moved on to better things of course, upgrading his house frequently, manipulating his finances and credit to buy the latest BMW or Mercedes and striving to make even more money by working longer hours further from home; an investment in a way, 'for a happy and eventual retirement' he used to tell anyone who asked. His eye was caught by a bee, busy on some dog daisies, and he smiled again. His pal, Bob, was an artist; my goodness was he good, why, his paintings of wild flowers were always on display at the school, no doubt that less than adequate 'Art' teacher bathing in the reflected glory of Bob's genius.

Every few years or so, when on business down that way, he would detour among quiet lanes to the secluded and still much untouched village of his childhood. Many of the other folk had moved on, as had he, but Bob was still there, still in the same old cottage, with its apple trees, vegetable plot and outside toilet. Bob was still the artist - and getting better every year too.

He smiled again and recalled how, on one visit, and over a cup of tea, he had asked Bob why he'd got that gnarled old bit of tree stump on his kitchen table; bits of soil and twigs and all. 'Why' Bob queried surprised, 'Can't you see the pool, the otters and their holt?'

A dismissive glance told him he could see nothing of the sort, just some dirty old lump of wood.

Well, next visit a couple of years later, the lump of unimportant wood long forgotten, he called on Bob for a chat about old and happy school days and a cup of tea and piece of home made apple pie, and there, on the table, was a wonder to behold.

Never in all his born days had he seen such a piece of work, never, ever, in all the galleries, museums and books, never, not ever. In differing and subtle shades of brown there were two playing otters, with bushes, rocks and pool, and even a fresh caught fish lay on the bank. The detail was so fine he wanted to gently stroke the otters to see if it was real fur and not wood. My goodness, did he want to buy this incredible symbol of life and beauty to display in his City home.

'How much Bob?' He asked eagerly.

'Sorry, old chum, not finished yet, lots to do, could take years, just can't tell,' replied Bob leisurely.

'But it's wonderful as it is, I will be the envy of all my friends. Name your price Bob, I'm not short of a penny or two', he implored.

'No, really', Bob insisted, 'I feel I've much more to do on this work'.

He reluctantly resolved to drop the subject, but not in his memory, for in the future, when it was finished, it would be his. He felt it would be worth waiting a whole lifetime for such a purchase.

It was about ten years before he again visited Bob and his old home village, he'd been very busy on many and very important business matters. Though he might have forgotten to visit, he had not forgotten the two otters sculpture, how could he?

'Come on in', welcomed Bob, 'sit yourself down and I'll stick the kettle on'.

Bob had not changed a bit, well, perhaps a little bit, he was a little thinner, losing some hair and had a slight stoop, but all the same it was still his good friend Bob inside.

He sat at the table wondering where his otter sculpture was, and at the same time admiring yet another, but quite smaller, masterpiece, a pool, a kingfisher and a butterfly all in perfect detail and harmony in wood. 'A fleeting image forever captured', he thought, 'truly beautiful.' 'Where's my otter sculpture, Bob?' He called across the kitchen in as positive manner as he could muster.

Bob replied with a childlike chuckle, 'You're looking at it, I found them there hidden inside the rocks and otters, kept the pool, couldn't see anything in it yet, water too muddy at the moment perhaps.' He chuckled again and poured the kettle water into his grandmother's old china tea pot.

What had Bob done? His dream, of owning the otters all for himself, was dashed, such perfection, gone, gone, and gone forever, no coming back, never, no not ever.

'May I buy this one off you please, Bob? He asked in a more humble and now subdued manner, remembering his previous attempt to buy Bob's work.

'Sorry old chap, not done yet, just a bit more, just a little bit more, not far to go now, getting near the end, soon be journey done,' rambled Bob.

It looked like a tear in Bob's eye, he thought, as Bob eased himself into the old wooden carver chair at the end of the pine table. Bob sipped his tea carefully, and then spoke like he'd not heard Bob speak before. 'Its all a journey you know, that's really the only bit that counts, the sculpture; you know, first you find something that appears to be nothing and you embark on a journey of discovery, and you find what you want not by collecting but by discarding, discarding the bits that aren't worth keeping and you end up with something truly beautiful, as your journey takes you further you find other bits that can be discarded to make it even more wonderful - and when finally you can discard it all , well , now then, that's enlightenment and your journey is over - the beauty of spirit is all yours and the original object, is long gone'. Bob sipped his tea again.

'Right', he said, 'very interesting', actually not really understanding a word. 'So when can I buy it then Bob?'

'When such a journey is finished, my old beloved childhood friend, it cannot be bought, for any money, by any person, the price was paid long ago by the traveller himself', he said with an air of knowingness and wisdom.

Back in the spring sunshine he half imagined he now understood what Bob had tried to say in his last ramblings. As his feet quietly crunched the gravel once more he overheard others talking. . . 'What a waste of such talent. . . could have made a fortune you know. . . could have been rich . . . they say he left nothing you know, not a thing he left. . . the cottage was rented and his furniture was the old stuff his parents had left behind. . . '

The voices faded into an obscure distance, and he thought, 'Maybe he took everything with him, or maybe he took nothing, and simply enjoyed to the full his time journeying on Earth. He journeyed his path with love in his soul and if anything was left by him it's going to be in us, and in how we now live our lives'.

His footfalls changed from gravel to tarmac and the sound of bird song to passing traffic. The great iron gates of the old town cemetery clanked shut behind him.

The Carpenter's Dream.

The fire crackled in the grate as the light of day faded at the old forest hut. The carpenter liked working alone, not least as it gave him time to engage in his spiritual adventures, the sort of activities that usually attracts the ridicule of others. He had faced this ridicule before and was, this time, going to live his dreams to the full. He read one last page of a treasured book he had picked up for a song at a village bazaar on the eastern edge of the forest. He could have had it for free but his nature was to pay his way, he believed everything had a price. It was a pity a few pages were missing but there was enough in what remained about the shadowy frontiers of dream realities to set his nerves tingling and fire his imagination for years to come. He had been particularly taken by the inscription, scrawled but readable inside the front cover;

'From ever living wood to paper,
from paper to words,
from words to mind,
from mind to wood.   I   Rubus
October 17th in the year of our Lord 1815 '.

He closed the book gently and placed it upon a table to his right, his hand resting a moment feeling the nurtured surface of old pine. Taking a sip of mulled wine to help him sleep he reflected on the passage he had just read. 'Could it really be we are alive in a dream of another's making or are we indeed merely dreaming we are awake? While we are in a dream it seems real enough, it is only when we seemingly awake that we cease to believe that dream reality and now believe in another. . . mmm,' he mused.

By the dying flicker of the fire he looked through the hut window into a darkening forest, 'indeed', he thought, 'if ever there was a place to find a real dream it would be here, in the moon-cast shadows of a great and ancient forest.'

He was not just a simple carpenter. You could easily mistake him for one who had lived many lives, even if only metaphorically speaking. He had travelled many lands, sought many teachers and punished himself physically in pursuit of an enlightenment that promised. . . well, he wasn't quite sure what it promised. His mind was still open on the matter, but he was sure as sure can be that there was something special he was destined to find; a something that might last forever perhaps.

He awoke to an incessant 'woo wooo' of the woodpigeons, set a small fire of well dried twigs collected from the forest floor and prepared his breakfast. Bacon, eggs and mushrooms, all in plenty in the pan, and somewhere at the back of his mind a 'something' gave thanks to the life of the pig that was lost and the life in the eggs that was never to be. He tucked in to his meal not knowing when he might get the next, for he had a plan to venture deeper into one of the steep wooded West Country Combes and could not be certain of the hour of his return. He knew he would travel far today but, ever hopeful, hoped his mind would travel further.

The dew had now gone and the hut was some miles behind him. His boots intuitively left the old path and, leaving the man planted rows of beech trees and their carpet of nut shells he entered an uncharted maze of oaks, beech, holly and silver birch.

Leaves had begun to fall and colours change. 'Looks like winter will come early this year', he thought. A surprised grey squirrel dashed quite unnecessarily for the safety of a great oak, as though its very life depended upon it. The prevailing wind off the rugged coast had help to shape trees in all fashions. As the carpenter looked at a particularly old and gnarled specimen he marvelled at just how tough trees grip onto life itself. He stood a short while thinking back to trees he had seen growing out of rock faces, and even once he had seen one on an old chimney stack.

He admiringly spoke quietly but out loud to this old tree: 'You never give up, do you? You might succumb to disease and, of course, old age will take you in time, but you never, ever give up, do you?'

A shaft of warm sunlight broke through the thinning valley cloud and warmed a fine mossy bank beneath the great tree. 'Time for a short rest from walking', he thought, 'and time for a little meditation'; for him a daily ritual. He unrolled the age softened green canvas that carried some tools of his trade and lay on it in the sun. 'Just like Kai lung's mat', he mused, and drifted into a day dream about who he, the carpenter, really was… Kai lung had written, 'it is well said of man that there are three of each of them. That which he is, that which he only thinks he is, and that which he intended to become'. For a short but unmeasured length of time he wondered how we can tell the difference between our three selves.

His mind drifted across the conscious and unconscious barrier between true reality, his perceived version of it and his dream world. This barrier he was determined to understand even though he had been warned that the harder he tried the more difficult it would become. Though he had met many great teachers he had found that they were often known as such only because they had somehow found and entered through their own spiritual door. The best they could do for him was to explain the path and hope he, the carpenter, might find his own door through which to discover enlightenment.

He believed he already held the 'key' to this door, ready for the allotted place and time of his own door appearing. He found the 'key' by following an old friend's meditation advice. 'Be the rock', Andy had told him, 'be the rock. Be still, in nature, be the rock, the rock does not think, it just is, the rock does not see, or hear, no need of food or breath, the rock just is. Be the rock and stillness is yours. Into the stillness from unknown dimensions the answer you seek will come. Be the rock.'

A shadow touched his hand. Rising, now fully refreshed, the carpenter stood and stretched his body in the warm sun. The Sun had moved some distance since he had stopped to rest at the tree. He chuckled to himself, 'yet another illusion', he thought, 'the Sun hadn't gone anywhere, it was where it was in the beginning, like the great truth I seek, it was always there, it is we that move.'

With a reverent pat and a silent goodbye the carpenter turned his back on the old oak and set off steeply down towards a stream. As he approached the gurgling waters there were what looked like human pathways, but experience told him that they were more likely to be the regular tread-ways of forest animals. It was many a time he had followed such tracks, usually to find they went somewhere he could not. 'Well, destiny comes not through chance but by choice', he reminded himself, and shaking himself out of a daydream he pressed onwards, on a path of his own making. Our carpenter had long believed that only one who risks is truly free, a belief that had many times taken him over new horizons.

What was he looking for, our carpenter? He was looking for a tree, a special tree in a forest of trees. He would know it when he saw it, just like when offered a pack of playing cards and asked to chose one, do we chose it or does it chose itself? Somehow, and is it not true, and for no known logical reason one of them will 'speak' to us silently and say, 'Me, me, pick me, I'm the one.' And so it was for our carpenter; a truly magnificent ancient beech tree that called to him in the quietness of the great void. It must have weathered the storms of centuries, its huge base trunk leaning towards the hill, as only living trees can do. What a beautiful specimen it was, though evidence of ancient damage abounded on it's trunk and larger branches, it wore a coat of smooth bark with wrinkles and shapes that sometimes looked like faces or animal heads. Like the tree, our carpenter had led a simple life. He owned no property of value, not even a watch to tell the time. 'What we deeply cling to, imprisons us', was a teaching that led him to a life of few associations and attachments, seeking only to do good and live out his path to enlightenment.

Placing his canvas bundle on the earth our carpenter stood under the leaning beech, his callused but gentle hand reached up and pressed against the trunk. In silence he offered the tree his respect and in some small way a brief rest from its labour of leaning. He pressed the centre of his palm firmly against the smooth bark and his feet responded by pressing into the earth, his back straightened and energy flowed. His breathing became fine, though deep and abdominal, and he visualised his feet sprouting roots that held him firm and centred. As time went by muscle aches came and went, and he worked on mentally strengthening the bones on which his ever relaxing muscles hung. The longer he held the posture the more he was able to drift in and out of that twilight zone between dream and reality.

Sometimes he felt that he was not there in the forest, sometimes reflecting on past lives and if trees had them too, sometimes seeing clear visions from earlier days to which he really felt that he had returned and, un-dream like, was indeed there. . .

In yellow writing on green in Sanskrit he read:

'Look to this day! For it is life, the very life of life. In its brief course lie all the varieties and realities of your existence, the bliss of growth, the glory of action, and the splendour of beauty. For yesterday is only a dream, and tomorrow is only a vision, but today, well lived, makes every yesterday a dream of happiness, and every tomorrow a vision of hope. Look well, therefore, to this day!'. . . (Kalidasa)

The Sun's shadows were now very long and a sense of mist growing in the air, our carpenter had found an enlightenment of sorts. He had felt communion with the spirit of the great tree, and whether real or not the carpenter felt that the tree had passed secrets of the ages to him. He had found his spirit and the great beech spirit could be one. . .

Time to leave and make the difficult but not impossible journey back to the hut and shelter, and of course his precious book, for now he realised he could make sense of the missing pages. Somehow his sleeping legs didn't feel like they belonged to him, almost a state of conscious mind but unconscious body, he was stuck fast, as though he really did have roots in the earth and as though the very bark of the tree had grown over his hand! In desperation he called to all the Gods, to white light, to anything, even begged the tree itself. He seemed to have entered the land of magic twixt reality and dream, and he knew not, the way out.

That winter came and went as did so many more; the forest passed into the hands of new owners, and the order given to clear the land was executed. Many fine trees went to the saw mill, but some of the odd shaped trees went to fire logs and some to toy manufacturers, who could use the shapes and grains to advantage.

A broad stump now stands as monument where once stood the great beech tree, a few shoots testament to its struggle for life, a legacy of the carpenter, perhaps. . .

                    The end. . . sort of. . .

The book?   Oh, it was used with kindling by the woodcutters at the hut.

The carpenter? Well, he was not seen again, but no one really missed him, after all he was always in one way or another somewhere else. In fact I don't think anyone ever looked for him.

The Beech tree? Ah, you have so many questions. Let me ask you. Have you ever had any wooden toys in the house? Did you ever talk to them as if they were human too? When woken by the creak of wooden boards, don't you ever wonder? Perhaps someone is trying to get in touch. . ..

Perhaps one day that wood will become paper and the paper a book, and the book will fill your mind with dreams and images of a great truth that you once thought was only found in fiction.

Fagus Sylvatica

22nd of December in the year of our Lord Two Thousand and four.

'Wake now or forever stay asleep'.

The Carpenter's return.
(Sequel to The Carpenter's Dream)

It was a cold winter's evening in the old town. Not far from the river, and beyond the old castle grounds and church, stood a special row, one among many, of early Victorian dwellings. One road above all stood out for its splendid brickwork and larger than normal buildings.

Old shoes clumped and brushed their way up the middle of this roadway in an otherwise silence. The road was empty of all but a heavy frost and one old black car parked outside the only house that seemed to have a light showing, and even then it was only a dim hallway light. Glazed, patterned floor tiles led to an ornate leaded glass door.

Shrugging his heavy coat about his shoulders, the owner of the shoes found himself drawn to the house, then to the door, then to the door bell. 'Dong, dong, dong,' it seemed to ring without him touching it. 'Strange', he thought, 'but not as strange as ee things 'ave appened afore this.'

An elderly fair haired woman of plainly obvious limited intelligence answered the door. 'Yus my dear', she said, 'what do you want?' The visitor came straight to the point of his calling, 'I'm looking for Jim Nightshade', he said. She looked visibly shocked, how could he have known about Jim. 'Wrong house luv, you want next door, number 46, you'll have to knock loud, as they'll be out back likely'. 'I'm zorry to trouble 'ee, and I thank 'ee for yer kindness, I bid 'ee good-night', he said. Then in the cold silence of the night he turned and made his way next door. He heard the old dear mutter something as she went back inside, it sounded like, 'Gawd save us mother', he thought, or something of that ilk anyway.

'Just as ee ole gal had prophesied', he thought, as a good 'thwack, thwack, thwack,' on the green painted door brought a cautious but inquisitive figure from the depths of the house to investigate.

A slim, strangely attractive woman with a look of the psychic about her held the door ajar and enquired, 'Yes?'

He was convinced she was inadequately hiding, as best she could, some knowing from him when he said, 'I've come to talk to Jim Nightshade'. In what appeared to him a somewhat strained voice she said, 'He used to live here once but has gone. . . you'd better come in, it's so cold out there'.

He kicked his old shoes against the step, as though by habit he was used to snow or mud on them. He lowered his green canvas bundle, leaving it on the porch tiles with his West Country accent and stepped into another world. A mixed world, 'Almost a place of dreams', he thought as he was led down a long hallway festooned with things of other times and places, some he thought he recognised as though he had been here before. They entered a room at the back of the house. ' This man is looking for Jim Nightshade', she said, keeping her back to him as she spoke to a distinguished, honourable looking man sitting by a large pine table. What our visitor thought to be long suffering eyes peered at him over a pair of narrow glasses. Some how the visitor felt an empathy with this man, who seemed kindly and hard working from his demeanour, was it the evident suffering. . . had he journeyed too, or perhaps he was a carpenter as well?

Having made the introductions the curious woman waited for her husband to speak.

'I'm afraid I've never heard of this Jim Whatsisname', the husband said, 'I'll put the kettle on for a cuppah'. 'Tea OK for you?' he asked from the kitchen door. . .

The visitor replied that tea would be fine and, if there was a biscuit going, it would be much appreciated as it was a long time since last eating.

Tea made, and a plate of biscuits on the table, they sat around the room, an open fire warming all it saw. All about them was the stuff of history, ancient furniture, ornaments of different ages, strange objects the like of which he had not seen before, and, looking down at him, several pairs of eyes. He thought one eye had winked at him, but put it down to the flicker of the wood fire in the grate. He even thought he saw the puppets on the shelves tremble as though excited to see him again, but he put that down to a draught from the open hallway door.

There was a short silence before they all spoke at once. . .

'You first', said the woman, even more curious than before. Our visitor agreed and at least now knew her name from hearing her husband ask permission to open the Tunnocks biscuits earlier.

'Well, Ducky, it's a long story, one of dreams, ancient teachings and spiritual searching, of self deprivation, misery and despair. It's something I don't think you'll be able to understand at your level'. He thought he heard an 'hmmph' sound from the husband but ignored it.

Ignoring the 'Ducky' bit, Sue, her real name, was keen to know why he was searching for Jim Nightshade. She knew exactly who and where Jim was but was determined it would remain a secret, 'So why do you want to speak to Jim Nightshade?' she demanded as politely as she could. Her husband rolled a thin cigarette, sipped his tea and entered a day dream of renovating his lovely old black car.

'Well,' he said thoughtfully, 'I've travelled the world, seen lots o' Masters, done some strange things and some downright frightening ones an' all, but in all my searching I found that true wisdom was to be found in the pages of a Pelham Puppet Club Book I found in a magazine rack in a Katmandu chiropractors.' He paused as if savouring the moment of his discovery, then continued, 'The Master's name was Jim, Jim Nightshade'.

His major work was 'Tales from the Dark Side'. . . he faltered and glanced up at the puppets whose wide eyes seemed to have fixed upon him, 'one of the truths beyond all truths, drawn from when time began', he continued, 'and I must find him and ask him about my dreams. I must find him.'

The husband stood from his chair, rubbed his knees and repeated that he couldn't help, 'Sorry old chap, this Tim Nightglade means nothing to me'.

The visitor wearily stood to take his leave when Sue, alias 'Ducky', exclaimed, 'Wait! I have an idea, it may not work but perhaps we can get in touch with Jim another way'.

The visitor stopped and looked hopefully; the husband sighed and sat back down on his chair.

Sue continued, knowing of course much, if not all, of what had been written in the tales of the dark side, 'I think a mini séance with beech wood puppets and puppets of the forest will bring you what you want'.

The husband stood again, rubbing his knees and resignedly offered to put the kettle on. 'Tea all round again, I take it'.

A candle was lit and around it sat the Beech wood puppets and those others entitled to be there; Red Riding Hood, the Wolf and the Woodcutter and so on. They sat intently as though it was they who had organised the event and lit the candle. The visitor joined them in the circle and Sue began an incantation to the spirit world.

Sue knew it would have to be a good act, but not so real that true spirits would overhear and enter their home.

She made it up the best she could, 'Ooo aarh oooo ah haa ooeeeeooo', she wailed, 'great spirits of the underhearth, spectra of the universe, we implore you, by the Roots of Trifidus Maximus and the Ladle of Achin Drum send us word'.

The visitor was a bit shocked, he'd seen some stuff before in his life, but this took the biscuit. He was to suffer even greater shock when she screamed out, 'Fagus, Fagus, is that you?'

How the devil did anyone here know my name, he thought, then blurted out, 'Yes, ar, tis I. Tis I'. It could only be Jim Nightshade, his Master, speaking, he thought.

In her best séance voice Sue asked, 'What is it you seek to know old wanderer?' Although intonation made it sound more like, 'what in the hell do you want round here?'

It was imperative Sue resolved the mystery in order to continue her clandestine work in the strange, eccentric world of puppet collectors, she had long considered number 46 to be a 'safe house' for hardened puppet fanciers, it was all now in jeopardy.

Fagus droned on, for what seemed like years, about strange dreams and the void between them and reality and perceived reality, about three of each of us but which was the real us, of mirrors and illusion and looking beyond that to true reality.

Sue couldn't listen to much more of this and her husband had gone from day dreaming about his car into an almost mesmerised coma-like state. It would have to end soon.

'Fagus, Fagus Sylvatica, cease your ramblings. I will tell you not of what you *wish* to know but of that which you *must* know'.

She needed to get rid of this visitor for good or at least shift his idolisation from Jim Nightshade. This was her chance. Fagus the carpenter stopped and listened, he was ready to hear the truth at last, he was about to find out if we can live and act out a life in the dream state, and if we can control it at will. At last, as he was ready to hear the great wisdom, he hardly noticed that the puppets' eyes were now all fixed on Sue.

'Oh Fagus, you have looked for the selves that cannot be found by mere mortals, you sought for that which can never be found by searching, and can only be found in stillness and non searching. In your search for the secrets of the great tree you trampled the twigs of joy that it placed at your feet. You must cease your wandering soul from its incursions into the wooded dreamland. I tell you, seek simple earthbound pleasures and be grateful you did not remain in the nether world of dream-wake when you communed with The Great Beech. Cease to guide others, for what use have they for a guide that is lost himself? Hear these words with your mind; do not let your ears listen alone. It is time for you to find a new way and a new home; it is your time now'. Sue had even amazed herself. At times it had been as though someone was talking for her, 'Still', she thought, 'let's hope it has worked a bit of magic'.

Fagus seemed to have taken it well, he smiled contentedly as if enlightenment was at last his, and thanked them both warmly for their kind hospitality, and he told them how lucky they were to live in such a special place surrounded by dear friends. 'It is my hope now to live out my life as such and cease my wanderings. I thank you muchly. I'll bid you a goodnight and *au revoir*'. So saying he went out briskly into the dark night air. He was gone in an instant into the darkness, gone too quickly from the dimly lit doorway to hear the shout, 'Hang on, you've left your bundle here'. They waited at the door for his return, but after a few minutes the cold was too much and they closed the door on the uninhabited night and carried the canvas bundle through to the cosy back room.

'We'd better open it', said John the carpenter, 'in case it's something important, then I'll go out and look for him, the silly old duffer'.

Sue agreed, she had always been a peculiarly curious woman, and now with a chance that Jim Nightshade wouldn't be found again she could relax.

The pine table was cleared and the canvas unrolled, at first came some beautiful chisels, the quality of which John had never seen before. He picked one up, 'Superb, absolutely superb,' he said. 'If Fagus doesn't return I would love to work with these, but I am sure he will come back, they are too precious. No carpenter worth his salt would be separated from them'.

Sue carefully unrolled the remainder of the canvas, they both gasped with delight, 'Oh John, look, it's a puppet, and so beautifully made. It's a carpenter and look he's got his own set of tools in canvas too'. Though when John looked there were no tools, just a canvas roll for effect.

'I didn't know Pelham made a carpenter', mused John. 'Well any way, we'd better look after it here 'til Fagus comes back, pop it up on the shelf with the others'.

It was late; they placed the fire guard, turned off the light and climbed the stairs to bed.

Meanwhile by the light of the dying fire, and sitting between Red Riding Hood and the Wolf, a contented Fagus took pleasure in his new home.

Taxus Baccata.
First day of January 2005

'The greatest hazard in life is to risk nothing. By not risking you are chained by your certitudes, and are slaves, having forfeited your freedom. Only one who risks is free.'

Zen Osho

Fagus' workshop; the story.

This is a long story, in fact, the longest of all, and could indeed entertain you for a lifetime, or maybe more than one. . .

In the old Beech copse the moss clad stones mapped out the ground like an ancient building. The stones and the tall trees welcomed in the group of tired walkers; they who had trod the Western Highlands in search of freedom and the chance to meet their soul on the path. She who was one with trees and animals beat gently the drum, 'bom', 'bom', 'bom'. Each found a place of solitude from each other but company with the trees. 'Bom', 'bom', 'bom', slowly, softly the drum beat reached out to the falling autumn leaves. The taller of the group, and not yet as insightful as others, sat on two flat stones he had heaped to make a comfortable seat. 'Bom', 'bom', 'bom', and the thinking mind was fading, like the sound itself into the distance, and the knowing, feeling inner mind became more alive, and alive to the great moss clad Beech Tree to his right.

As the earthly surroundings faded he became aware that a moss covered arched door had opened in the tree and the diminutive figure of Fagus beckoned him in. Inside it was so roomy and was well lit with firefly and glow-worm lanterns, it was warm and dry with an earth floor and a large central walnut table on which Fagus poured two cups of tea. 'A rare thing this', Fagus said, 'Not much walnut of this age left any more. One of the best things I've ever salvaged from man's above earth destruction. Still, that's enough of that. How did you get here?' The tall traveller eased his bones with a stretch and said, 'I have come far, from beyond the Great Bog Territories, raging torrents, and climbed the great hills where one can fly across the valleys'. Fagus smiled, 'A brave journey my friend', he said, 'Did you come alone?'

After a sip of tea and a longing look at some ginger cake that Fagus had just placed on the table he replied, 'No, we are five, though not here all together, one has stayed to nurture her toes and investigate the valley buildings where we stay. Our guide is patient and strong like a lioness, and such is her power that no bog or hill could bar her way; it is she that led us to your door. The location of the key, unknowingly hidden inside our very selves, was given to us by her friend, a joyful little woodland fairy we know as Maggie. She teases the secrets from our souls and communes with rocks and trees and they with her.'

Another sip of tea and a good chunk of ginger cake later he continued, 'Also one of five is a friend and fellow traveller but she is one who has journeyed afar and in other times methinks. While others sleep she walks the dark as quiet as starlight and guards the resting with her compassion'.

'But enough of us,' said the traveller, 'How have you been keeping, I heard that the old house in Bedford is now empty and no knowing what became of those who were, and what are you doing in this hollow tree?' 'Aha,' said Fagus, chuckling to himself, 'This is my workshop. You remember of course that I was a carpenter in a former life; well I continue my work in this one. When the old house was sold the puppets were sent to new masters but I was lucky when the postman failed to notice my parcel fall from his bicycle not far from here and the house to which I was to be confined in slavery as all puppets are. Didn't you know why trees are hollow? It's because we take the wood and make beautiful things with it. If we're good at our job we can get to the great trees before man'. Curious to know how this was possible the traveller asked, 'Then where do all the shavings go, and where are the beautiful things?' 'Well,' Fagus replied, 'You in the upper world have discovered that atoms consist mostly of vast amounts of empty space, but you didn't know this until you desired and knew how to look, so it is down here, the great void, another dimension, an alternate wavelength, the abyss, Valhalla, call it what you will, for it matters not, only that it is so. It is in this space Earth's great treasures lay.'

Again a broad grin spread across Fagus' face, 'I think it is now safe to tell you, for you have begun to open your heart to the 'knowing' and in any event when you tell others, as you surely will even if asked not to, they'll never ever believe you, and that is why we are safe down here, for only those who truly care will ever truly know'.

An excitement coursed through the traveller's body like some ghost was trying to occupy it. 'At last', he thought, 'I'm going to be told the great secrets of life'. 'Not so fast', said Fagus reading his mind, 'I can show you the way but it is only your own effort that will take you on the path, step by step and one foot in front of the other. No one can walk it for you, for then it would only have value for them alone and not for you'. The traveller mused on these words and thought earlier of the trek to Glomach Falls where mountain water dived unhesitant 350 feet into the valley below, a magnificent and awe inspiring sight, but for the eyes to see this at all their feet had to carry them there.

'Now!' Fagus said seriously, 'Come', and he beckoned to the side of a buttress like inner support of the tree to reveal a set of steps. 'These steps', confided Fagus 'are the steps to the infinite space below ground where all Earth's treasures are stored'. 'But I can only see one step,' exclaimed the traveller.

'The first step is one of *'fear'* and stops you seeing others,' comforted Fagus, 'Here, take my hand and your fear will be lessened.' He took the open hand and it was true, he was not quite so afraid, though he realised then that the steps were so narrow that sometimes it would have to be single file, and would the fear return? Indeed, once the fear had subsided, the other steps down were easier to see.

Fagus led the way, carrying a lantern just bright enough to see a few steps at a time. 'Be warned', cautioned Fagus,

'Concentrate your whole being on one step at a time, do not let your eyes or your mind wander to those that may be in the future, any slip and you may fall into the abyss and for ever be in a dark place without the knowledge to find the light that frightens away the demons of fear and despair.

Our traveller took the first step, banging his head on a little wooden sign hanging from ivy string above the narrow doorway. Though the sign was in some ancient script he found he could read the message, 'Without risk you are chained to your past.' 'Mind your head' Fagus warned belatedly, 'Now remember, you must feel the step you are on, not rooted in the past or dreaming of a future that may not come, every part of you should be in the 'now', and trying to absorb the essence of the one step through the very soles of your feet.' 'Thinking has no place down here, only feeling'. 'Now, let me see, what it is the next one is about. . . aha, of course . . . . *Faith*'. 'Now Faith is believing in something that you cannot prove but that you accept exists, you may not have seen the proof but others have, and in the great connective consciousness they will reach out to you and transfer belief by their presence alone. Just like the blackbird that can sing its heart out even while the dawn is still dark. Don't be confused, for later you will find a step for acceptance and one for belief and one for understanding and yes the last step will be . . . ? . . . we will both know what it is when you find it.'

The traveller absorbed '*Faith*' into his being, how could he deny faith otherwise he could not be here. Were not faith and overcoming fear connected? Come to think of it weren't all the steps connected? He hoped so, in more ways than one, for he could not see what held them up. Fagus, seemingly now losing his endless patience, snapped, 'What have I told you about looking forward and here you are thinking and not feeling and to cap it all using words from other steps like '*hope*' and '*connection*'. There will be a place for anticipation when you're actually on its step.' Fagus continued, 'Just stop your talking for once and listen and feel, let me tell you what it is you need to know.'

'Phew, snappy little so and so', the traveller thought and then realised that he'd done it again. He took a deep breath and began to try and sense the meaning of the step.

'There are a couple of quick steps here old friend, quite easy to take in', Fagus kindly assured the traveller, feeling somewhat guilty for his little outburst; Though he did think that at times it could be justified where life and death were in the balance. 'This one is *Value* and *being valued*. In the great scheme of the Cosmos what is it that we touched in life on which we would put a high price? You must feel this for yourself. . . And what of being valued? Do we need it?' Fagus paused a long pause, 'Well done old friend, you sense it right, if it was done for the right reason we have no need to experience being valued for it'.

They moved down the steps into an ever deepening sense of darkness, though the occasional glint of quartz crystal in the earth walls reminded him of the bright stars in an indigo sky. It made the traveller realise you could 'see' remote things without going beyond where you stood.

That brief feeling went as Fagus told him, 'Rest again here on the step of *'accomplishment'*, and for a short while you may reflect on the feelings you have felt. . . Pay heed now for the path does not always go so easily, there may be danger ahead. Carefully place the feet on each step without stumble, for that will take your mind and disturb your journey. A bit like stubbing your toe, your mind is in the toe and all feelings relate only to that and leaving little space for other, better, feelings to enter your being. Therefore walk carefully and with mindfulness or the treasure of the Earth stored in the great under-space of the infinite will never be yours. How often have you come to understand something but cannot recall by which route you came to it? Well, the step is the same, having trod the step it is hard to imagine how you arrived or indeed that you were not always there.

Down, down, and down, step by step, knees tightening with tension, but senses more alive than ever, warmth and tingling in the hands and feet, downwards they went.

'Whoa!' shouts Fagus, with what appeared to be a tiny gloating and knowing smile. 'Watch out for this one, it was put in by mistake, so they say, and is difficult to remove, so they say. Many times you'll tread this step and without true awareness not realise you are there.'

'Damn', thought the traveller, 'That 'Ego' step felt so good, it had me fooled for something substantial like. . .' He couldn't think of anything it was exactly like, he was beginning to learn how subtle were the changes in feeling, perhaps you can come up with an answer when you tread this step yourself. On the step of 'questioning' Fagus allowed the traveller to speak again. 'I'll tell when it's OK or not', Fagus said. The traveller inquired 'Will this path lead to the 'Great Truth'?

Fagus laughed a friendly little laugh, 'Why, no, there is no 'one truth' only 'a truth' just as there will never be certainty, you must just do the very best you can in all circumstances, to be the truth and not seek it for it is not out there beyond self to be found'. Down, down, down, the space underground seemingly now so vast. Fagus, like some people can, picked up on his feeling and said 'We have touched on this before, but we are all mostly space, this was known to the ancients long before scientists discovered what they called the atom and discovered a tiny planet surrounded by comparatively massive space, and little things with no mass at all charging round the edges like crazy. Some feel that travelling the steps allows us into that dimension where space, true nothingness, exists in the forever now. Some people can see images or colours that others cannot and this is a similar idea, though not at the same level; however it fits the principle of entry to another dimension and therefore awareness of a different wavelength. Perhaps for a brief moment they have unknowingly trod some steps, with their relaxed mind crossing into the subconscious. The subconscious of course knows all but keeps the secret until the step is trod, then, if there is mindfulness to access the secret, it is revealed. It's what you humans call inspiration or sometimes, rashly, enlightenment.

Of course, there are sadly too many that have embraced the dark pleasures like the Ego we met earlier. The traveller interjected, forgetting his earlier resolve and said, 'Perhaps they've not had such a noble, all knowing, angel spirit like you to guide them through their own inadequacies.' Fagus replied with a chuckle, 'Of course, you are right, I am wonderful.'

He laughed again, they both laughed, the infinite space heard and echoed their laughter, and they were on the step of '*humour*' and it felt good.

Laughter stopped as suddenly as it started and a feeling of foreboding filled the traveller, for he had sensed what Fagus was about to say about the next step. 'You'll love this one', Fagus said, with only half a smile left, 'This narrow, rickety one is 'trust'. When you step out on to this one you'll feel like you might fall, and the abyss below seems to look into you and draw you down. Trust may only be a small step, but a really big one in terms of where it can take you, if you know what I mean. Try not to lean or use your hands, stay upright, it's the best way'. The traveller did have trust, he trusted Fagus, but he also trusted his instinct too, and that thin wobbly step looked like it should not be trusted. How deceiving appearances can be. He searched his soul for the lesson gained on the step of 'fear' and made his move. How glad he was that he had trusted, for he now felt more secure than ever before in his life. He stretched out his arms wide into the emptiness and with palms facing downwards to meet the uprising energy of the void he felt that he could not fall, for how can one that flies ever fall, he knew what it was to be the eagle.

'Come on,' urged Fagus, 'let's keep moving, so many more to go. Of course, you know that even great Masters are still learning till the day they die, and if the path is too hard for you, you can always turn back; trouble is if you do you will return to a world where you always get what you always got. It's up to you, and this is where to do it. . . '*Decision'.*' It was an easy and comfortable step, made so because it was taken with no thought but feeling, ninety nine per cent correct is our instinct, we just don't listen to it. Everything in the traveller's body told him it was right to continue, for he'd gained so much in so little time compared to the years of struggle and sacrifices which had previously brought him little. 'Next step now', he thought, and he knew already what it was, he was becoming more sensitive. It was the *'thinking'* step. He whispered to Fagus, so as not to break the rules, and just in case someone or something else was listening, 'Thinking step Fagus. . . thinking destroys feeling. . . thinking takes a long time but understanding and feeling they come like magic in an instant.' Fagus knew he could relax more now for the traveller would soon be able to find his own way, and though he would always remember the guide he would safely walk his own path into a brighter future.

But not just yet, and he led the traveller down, down, down, through the feeling steps. The step of *'now'* , where he reminded the traveller of earlier words of 'not forward, not back but the step you are on', and how most accidents are the result of an out of now experience; walking into a lamp post for example. (The traveller wondered how Fagus could have known, for he had done this very thing - more than once as it would happen!) Yogis and the like experiment with the 'now' and touch the essence of knowing, often with breath technique. Fagus had explained, 'breathe out and hold it out, until forced to breathe it in, that space between is the closest you can truly feel to a now moment, for nothing but that moment has any significance, not past, not future, but only now.'

'Now,' said Fagus, 'remember I told you we would come to *'anticipation'* all in good time, well here it is; now you may look forward.' Pleased to have arrived where he was allowed a look to the future, the traveller anticipated the final step. Would it be enlightenment, or happiness, perhaps just being, or would it be to return to the beginning and know for the first time? He found he could anticipate the step but not what it would bring. Fagus eased his torment and said, ' Don't try to work out what the final step is, you won't know it until you arrive, and in the same way you'll find a disappointment in not being able to share your discovery with others. It will mean nothing to them; you waste your breath, for you cannot walk their steps for them. Your conscious mind can never know when all the steps are trod, just as you cannot know the steps of others, for they too will be different and our journey may end before the path is run.'

So they moved on to the step of *'story telling'*, oh how the traveller wanted to stay here, desperate to tell of 'The Princess and the China Bell' with its new happy ending, perhaps you'll hear it when you are on this step, but there was no time to linger, just time to know this step existed, many great writers and readers too are trapped on this step and are happy enough to be there. 'No time for that now', said Fagus, 'I want you to spend more time with this one, for it reveals much more than it conceals if you know how to see. The traveller stepped forward eagerly but was held back by a firm hand, 'Careful old chap'' warned Fagus, 'We will sit on this step together with our feet firmly on the step below it, the step of 'awakening' and the step we sit on is the step of *'dreaming'*. Remember well these words 'wake now or forever stay asleep', and when you sense the sign to wake make sure you act, for it has great purpose. The sign may be a voice or a vision or sometimes an urgent sounding knock, knock, knock. Make sure you wake!' The traveller did not need to be told twice about this warning; he had in the past ignored such things until a fearful apparition was sent to stand in his home to make sure he paid attention. He looked straight in Fagus' eyes and said with deadly conviction, 'Don't worry Fagus, I'll not be staying asleep!' Trouble is with dreams is you can't tell what is real or not, nor how long the dreamtime kept your consciousness, you might vision an epic but it took only seconds of waking time, or perhaps the other way round. The dream world has immense power that often will not transfer to the waking world. In dreams there are questions and answers too of great intellect and intricacy which are beyond the wit of the woken mind that dreamed them. Songs may be sung with beautiful words the like of which are yet to be written, and colours so bright and clear that even the finest stained glass window cannot surpass. As the sub conscious shuffles the cards of places, people and deeds we can have no inkling of the hand to be dealt.

There is no doubting when to wake as you physically feel or hear the signal, the only question is, how important it is to you! No knocking on windows or doors this time, no gentle ghost like shaking of the feet, but a gentle 'bom', 'bom' , 'bom' in the distance. The traveller was wide awake now and Fagus next to him, just sitting expressionless, being the watcher. 'Well?' asked Fagus, 'what did you see, eyes closed or not in your dream?' 'Was I asleep for long?' inquired the traveller. Fagus confided, 'It's not important, old friend, it's the message that is, not how long it took to arrive! The dream may have lasted but a split second and it might take you a day to describe. That should give you a sense of the immense power of the subconscious when it is allowed to operate in the now. So, let's hear your dream and when you have finished you will have arrived at the next new step'.

'Strewth!' exclaimed the traveller, 'where to start? There was so much, so much colour, I could feel the weather and hear the bird song. I'm sorry if I miss bits out, but I'll do my best'. He continued, 'We had just taken a step, one you warned me of earlier for thinking ahead but said we'd come to eventually, 'connection' . I stood alone, but not lonely, at an ancient burial site of it seemed some 4,000 years , and which was bounded by Beech trees,; huge stone mounds marked the spot where an ancient was lain to rest by his fellows in evident respect and honour. His body and tomb, salted with again the quartz crystals, aligned to the Sun of the Winter Solstice. Each tomb too had a circle of standing stones, one of which I placed a hand either side to see if palm to palm energy could penetrate the rock. . . and it did too!. In this special place a feeling came to me that my soul was connected with all other souls, for the spark of life is from a universal source.

I felt wonder for those ancients that possessed a knowing, long since lost by modern man, but I could only feel the energy of self and that of the gentle rain dashed wind that blew. It came to me that some of us will ever sense nothing significant at such a place and others will ever feel the presence. This presence may be the pulse of Mother Earth or sometimes a travelling soul on the low road beneath. Souls on the low road would often confide their secrets to the trees, the connectors of earth with the heavens, and oft times humans will confide in a tree and oft times too the tree with them, and so the folk lore lives on that trees have wisdom. One of the great Beeches silently called me to sit at its feet; it was much like the one we are now below. As the thinking mind began to fade and the watching mind gain in presence I saw an eye with my closed eyes and knew for the first time that the eyes we see are fleeting glimpses of the watcher inside, and some times other watchers from other parts of the great universal soul consciousness come too, for they too must watch. There was something about the number of steps was the same as number of stones on the burial mound, I think but am not too sure about it now. If only stones could talk we could find out.'

The traveller seemed to be dreaming again, for he sensed Fagus had gone, he heard a sound like a door closing behind him forever, and the soft 'bom', 'bom', 'bom', came gently on the breeze to his ears, and the dappled shade of the copse met his eyes, and he was no longer sitting on the step of dreams but on the little stone seat he had made earlier. 'Time to head back now', said the guide, 'not many steps left before we are home once more, and back at our beginning.'

I could tell you more, but I've said too much already, sshhhsh. . . listen. . . listen carefully. . . Did you not hear a knocking just then. . . ?

Salix Caprea October 2005

'Do not seek to follow in the footsteps of the wise, seek what they sought.'

Adventure

The Victorian Fireman's Axe.

An adventure story interwoven with facts and told from the perspective of the axe itself.

We were such good comrades, that old fellow and me; constant and dependable companions; we'd been together for over thirty years; we'd faced death and disaster many a time, side by side; the crumbling stairs, the choking acrid fumes; just a way of life for us both.

I suppose, in a way, we were both forged in fire. He was born around 1874 and I in 1878. We worked together in a small but industrious little estuary town. The tidal river ebbed and flowed carrying various cargoes for the warehouses not so far from our station and many a time the firemen would pick up a few 'silver darlings' for dinner from the herring fishers on the quay.

Though it wasn't a big station it had seen many changes, even whilst I was there. The horses and 'steamer' were still there when I started, the place was heated by a coal fired boiler and there were various outbuildings storing hay and the like - I never went in there myself, had no need of me I suppose - but others told me how it was.

Though the place was somewhat Spartan it was clean. Twice daily the tile-red painted floor was washed and was clean enough to eat off; the brass work of door bell, steps, fire door mechanisms and all the equipment was so polished you could see to shave in - not that they did - many of the men had fine sets of whiskers. A row of polished brass helmets rested on hooks above smart, collarless double breasted tunics - the sort of tunic that inspired every man to stand tall and proud that ever felt its fit. It was with this tunic I would wait, waiting for the bells to go down and my comrade to come and fetch me.

For a few years, until he died of old age, a scruffy stray brown dog was adopted by the station. They used to laugh a lot at his antics, but admired greatly the dog's courage so close to fires; I think they called it 'Braidwood', though I cannot tell you why, but it did seem to amuse the firemen greatly. Anyway, that dog lived the life of Riley, (whoever that was), and was well fed and slept by the boiler, then when the alarm sounded would run out into the street and follow the men to the fire. What a life, what a lucky old thing, ah, how I envied that dog.

Where was I? Ah, yes, change. The station was to have the new electric light, and later, though the big brass hand bell still hung on its bracket, we were to have a big electric bell fitted. Every few years the station would be sent a new pumping appliance, (those on the outside, who I was informed knew nothing, called them fire engines). The old one would be polished and cleaned with pride as it would be sent to a less busy station, and we had a reputation to honour. The new one would take its place and result in a flurry of activity, starting it up, stopping it, starting it up, pumping water, men running with hoses and ladders with lots of shouting going on from the watching silver helmeted officers. My comrade never wanted to be one of those officers, it just wasn't for him, for he had a deep sense of duty which he felt was only truly satisfied at a place the men called, 'the sharp end'. For this I am eternally grateful as it's the only place I can work. He was good at what he did, come to think of it, so was I, we were a formidable team, us two.

Then, one day, he didn't come in to work; I was placed alongside some boots and on top of some folded uniform and fire tunics, then taken by the Brigade wagon to a place I later learned was called 'brigade stores'.

After all my valiant and unstinting service I was to be incarcerated, in a small dark room, in a box.

Occasionally the door would be opened and, along with the store man's hand, light would come in and bring a glint to polished and waiting steel. The hand would fumble then select from the box, and one of us would be taken. Sometimes the choice was rejected and the 'un-chosen one' was thrown at the back of the tiny wooden room, never to be allowed back with us in the box. We, who had given so much to change the destiny of others, were now uncertain of our own. Sometimes, when this door was opened we could see young men in new uniforms, with buttons bright and thick black polished leather belts. One time, when the door was left open by accident, we saw one of our brothers, a chosen one, being handed to one of these keen smart young men. He grasped the ash handle and made some amateurish chopping action with the blade. It amused us - he would learn. He was only young and now he had one of us to look after him - to stop him sliding down a slate roof to his death, to open locks that barred his way, to quick release the pressure in a snaking hose dangerously out of control, oh, so many things our brother would show him. He put the axe in his belt, the cupboard door was closed. We were never to see either of them again.

It seemed forever that we stayed in that small wooden prison. When all was quiet outside and the store-men home to bed we would share our stories. . . of action, of noble strength and relentless courage; like our comrades we were prepared to do all that was required and to make sacrifice when duty beckoned. We often wondered why, when we had served so well, and given so much, what we had done to deserve a fate such as this. Strange, but one morning, about lunchtime, we overheard the store-men discussing the state of an axe that had been returned much the worse for wear, chipped blade, scorched handle. Finally we heard, 'If only they could talk, what stories they could tell us. . . ah, well, . . . I'm afraid it's in the bin with you,' and so saying, the store-man dropped our valiant brother into the rubbish. Too bad the cry for mercy fell on deaf ears.

Just think, if only they knew of the stories that were being told, just a few feet away.

I well remember telling my brothers one cold night about the last shout I went on with my old comrade. . .

It was a deadly dark and bitterly cold November night, a winter wind pattered sleet on the dormitory windows, it was the last of our twenty four hour duty shift and tomorrow would be a rest day. Then, in the wee hours of the morning, the big six inch electric bells burst fearsomely into life. Men, forced by duty, habit and a shock of adrenalin leapt up from their beds, blankets cast aside and eyes wide staring open as they rushed for the rest of their fire fighting uniform.

They could smell the smoke filling the air as they prepared themselves to turn out, the driver strenuously hand cranking the petrol engine into life. Two more men pulled the thick ropes that folded open the great red doors of the appliance room, and they looked into the winter street to see by the light of the engine's lamps a mixture of driving sleet and billowing thick, yellowed smoke.

They knew, tonight of all nights, this was indeed a working job they had on their hands.

It wasn't far to go, just down the road at one of the old wharf buildings that backed on to the river.

It was a hotch potch of a building, part stone , part brick, that had been added to many times over the years, making a labyrinth of secret places the demon fire could sneak unseen to trap and cut off the unwary. It was a building of three floors and part basement, about one hundred yards deep and about thirty yards wide. It was used mainly for storage of mixed goods, almost anything could be there, wool, timber, grain, jute, anything; the fire seemed to be located on the second floor and was 'showing a light', flames being visible through breaking windows. The Sub Officer had himself and six men; he sent two of them quickly away to locate and set in to a hydrant, the pump man stood by the controls. The Sub pointed and shouted his orders, 'take a line of hose around to the windward side and play the jet through any windows on the second floor. . . Break them if you need'. . . and two more men were gone, along with their heavy canvas hose, into the dark. Now they were three, 'Right,' he said, trying to sound confident but deep down knowing this to be a daunting task, they would need the Angels with them tonight, 'Come with me; we'll have a quick look inside. Bring a couple of lamps; let's go'.

So close we were to the fire and so far we were from help, it would be twenty minutes at least before another crew might arrive, we were on our own.

The main door was padlocked against us, it was a job for me and I didn't hesitate, with my brave but aging comrade … a tough steel point through the hasp and a wrench of the ash handle and the lock was in two. Just as we took our first wary footsteps through the doorway one of the men from the hydrant reported back, out of breath, gasping, 'line in from hydrant, Sub, but jet's hardly reaching second floor!'

The town only had a two inch diameter water main and the pressure was never much good at the best of times. There were no ponds and any wells in the vicinity would not last a jiffy.

The Sub seemed to stare into the air as if looking for an answer, then, realising something must be done quickly or the fire might spread to other buildings, as already sparks and glowing embers were being carried in the wind, he made his choice, (as we also must make our choice in time), he shouted loud, above the roar of the fire now competing with the roar of the engine running nearby, 'Right!' 'Get our pump moved to a corner in case the building comes down, find any one in the street that can help you and set into open water, get a second jet to work'. As the man turned to leave, the Sub shouted, 'and take him with you, get going!' This left just the Sub Officer and us two. I think he kept my comrade with him for a couple of reasons, firstly to save him from all that heavy, heavy work setting in to open water with that awful cumbersome rubber and wire suction hose, and secondly because of all the years of experience and knowledge that could prove invaluable inside this growing inferno.

'Come on', shouted the Sub, 'let's find the stairs'.

It wasn't long before we found them, they were made of stone, not good news this, stone stairs had been known to collapse without warning; give us timber stairs any day, you knew where you were with them. The noise increased as we made our way ever upwards, so great was it that we didn't hear the call from below. 'No water!' The tide was out, too much mud. . .

The crew fell back to setting in to the hydrant, exhausted and covered in cold mud from their exertions to reach the water's edge. They had, however, improved water supply by shipping another standpipe into a water main a street away.

The crackling jet was now beginning to play through an open window, quickly turning to steam and occasionally hitting a glowing cast iron pillar, one of many that supported the floor above.

Sharp and very hot slates were now cracking and sliding off the roof to the ground below, tiny holes sprung leaks in the canvas hose, the crew with the jet sheltered as best they could. They didn't know what else to do; they could only but follow the last order. They waited amongst the falling debris for assistance to arrive or their Sub to return.

'What a bloody mess', cursed the Sub officer, as we surveyed the stacked goods of the first floor as timbers above creaked and the sound of falling slates and spalling stonework filled our ears, 'If only we could salvage some of this. . . but. . . just the two of us. . .' His voice trailed off, then, 'what the hell was that?' The Sub stared at us disbelievingly. We had heard it too. It was a scream, almost inhuman in nature. 'For God's sake', the Sub gasped, 'there's someone up there; what the hell are they doing here?'

'Night watchman, that'll be my guess Sub,' said my comrade in a serious but calmly measured manner, 'it'll be old Fred, he's got a gammy leg. . . that's why they gave him this job. . . I'm pretty sure I can find him Sub.'

'Go for it then, take care, you damn well come back safe; I'll check on what's happening outside and get help in to you as soon as it's possible', with that said, the Sub Officer's strong and dirt ingrained hand patted him admiringly on the shoulder and in an instant he had melted away down the dark stairs to the ground floor.

I had a moment to reflect on this. . . what did my comrade mean, 'I'm pretty sure I can find him', what happened to the 'we', after all we wouldn't have even got this far without my help. Then I realised I'd fallen into the old ego trap, I'd forgotten that what endeared us most to the Brigade was adherence to our motto, *'Service without praise for eternity'* it brought us the greatest of respect and status. We asked for nothing but to be allowed to serve, we were almost invincible.

We found the next stairs, now of timber, and had to brave a small fire on our way upwards.

I tell you, I remember thinking, 'I hope he knows what he's doing!'

Frantically, and beginning to choke in that killing air, we searched for old Fred; we found an open rear window and looked out and down, there in a crumpled heap on the flags below lay the reason for the scream, it was indeed old Fred. Just out from the window to the right was an old cast iron rainwater down-pipe; when young and fit it is quite possible to climb down such as this if you know how. Perhaps Fred had considered this his only way out; it was a young man's game that, even for us it looked decidedly dangerous, and we'd done it before. We turned to leave but that demon fire had sprung its trap and spawned such living destruction and chaos behind us that now *we* must find another way out!

Water sprayed in through a broken window on the far right side; with plaster off the walls in places, timbers creaking and bits of broken slate peppering the floor we made our way across, at least there some fresh air came in. My dear comrade gulped in some clean air then called out to the men below. At first they could not hear him but then they did, almost everything was dropped as they rushed to retrieve the wooden ladder. . . we could hear the orders snapping out apace, we knew they would be here soon. . . 'head away. . . extend. . . well. . . lower. . . under run. . . heel to building. . .'

A panting, red and whiskered face suddenly appeared at the window. . . 'Bloody bars! . . . 'Bloody barred windows!' . . . 'Give us yer axe 'ere and I'll try and break one free!' I was quickly passed out through the broken glass into slippery new hands still numb from the soaking cold of holding hose and branch.

I fell; clonk, clonk, clonk as I hit the rounds of the ladder on the way down, accompanied by a panicky bawled cry of 'stand from under!' I heard the heavy fire boots thumping down the ladder. . . 'pawls, step out!' screamed the now shocked and solitary fireman footing the ladder, then I was passed from hand to hand and we returned to the head of the ladder, at first he shouted out to my brave comrade that all would be well, that we were back and he wasn't alone anymore. Using my chisel-shaped spike he hacked at the stone work that held the bar in place. There was no voice from inside, there was no sign from inside and I wondered if he had gone back to try the drainpipe. . . all we could see from outside was the deep red glow of a big fire in a sea of choking smoke, then it happened. . . Whether it was the roof that gave in or the hot gases had ignited - suddenly all hell broke loose and searing hot gas and flames appeared at every window with a loud but dull 'crump'. The fireman on the ladder was forced to duck down and away from the window to save himself. He climbed quickly down shouting, 'get some water in through that window - quick - for God's sake. . .'

The Sub Officer turned up, extra crews had arrived, water supplies had been improved and progress was being made.

My comrade? I don't know, I heard others talking. . . 'he must have found another way out'. . . and another say, 'yeah, if any one could, he could. I wouldn't be surprised to see him come out that front door any minute.'

I didn't hear or see any more as the initial crew were relieved and sent back to station and I with them. They made a pot of tea, opened the door of the boiler and stared silently, with both hands clutched around hot mugs, in their wet clothes, at a fire that was now not their enemy but their friend. I remember thinking, as we warmed up safe in our station, 'I pray he's alright.'

Dawn was beginning to break and a new day to begin.

Well you know the rest, I can't imagine anything bad happened to my comrade, if it had I should have been with him, the guilt is still in my heart that I didn't stay with him, if only I hadn't slipped. . . sorry, excuse me a moment. . . I just can't think that.

I've been to many places since being forged in the fire, and I can still do today what I could do one hundred years ago given the chance. I spent many wasted years lost and alone in various cupboards, and for the last ten I've been an ornament

on a shelf in a retired fireman's home - I don't think his wife likes me - hang on, here she comes now with that damned duster and polish. . . must stop now. . . thanks for listening - not many give me the chance you know. . . if only they would. . . that's all we ever needed. . . just a chance. . .

§

Notes:

Silver darlings. . .	Herrings.
Steamer. . .	Coal burning and steam driven pump used by the fire brigade
Braidwood. . . .	an early and most practical and heroic Chief fire officer (actually died at a building collapse, he was renowned for his tactics of close quarter attacks on fire)
Jute. . .	a vegetable fibre often also called Hessian.
Jet. . .	the jet of water issued from the branch - the brass metal nozzle at the end of the fire hose.
Pawls step in. . .	Where extensions of ladders were held in place by pawls there would be an overlap, this instruction would be shouted to the man climbing the ladder to warn him of their proximity.
Stand from under. . .	Any time an object was lowered or accidentally dropped from above this shout would be given to warn colleagues below. Training and experience meant they never looked up to see what it was!
Sub Officer. . .	A Junior Officer who would command a crew at operational incidents and day to day running of the station.
Hydrant. . .	basically the big tap in the water main into which firemen could 'ship' a standpipe and obtain a flow of pressurised water.

THE MAROON
A lifeboat adventure story.

Some few years past now and engulfed in a cold mid December, the little fishing village was entombed in a deathly dark and stormy night; a heavy fist thumped hard on the coxswain's cottage door; and thumped again, and thumped again, though mostly drowned out by clattering rain, howling wind, the roaring sea and a roll of thunder.

The coxswain, well respected in the village and popularly known as 'old Bob', was not a man to dilly dally, and in his heart of hearts he'd had a feeling this would happen. His door soon opened, spilling light into the foreboding gloom and there it fell on the rain drenched faces of two ... no ... three men.

No need to ask what was wanted, their presence said it all; the nearest, an old fisherman called Dave, gasping for breath shouted, 'Yacht. . . big one. . . off sand bar. . . looks like she's in. . . big trouble!'

Without a word spoken, old Bob threw on his big coat, pulled the door closed behind him and all four hurried along the narrow cobbled street into the enveloping darkness and towards the lifeboat station. No words were exchanged, but many a thought ran through their minds, ' tide's in', 'wind's nor easterly, off the sea', 'will we get a crew?' 'Can we launch in this messy sea?' 'Whose is she?' 'what the hell's she doing out there in this storm?'

A stabbing flash of lightning reflected brightly off the rain lashed cobbles and lit up an old stray dog cowering in the half shelter of some cottage steps. The village seemed deserted, windows closed and shuttered against the relentless rain.

They were soon at the station; breathless they went about their tasks in silence, each knew what they must do. Lights flickered on all over the station, the radio crackled into life, and the coxswain went to look at the slipway - now almost hidden by crashing waves. 'Not enough crew', he shouted, 'get a maroon off!', and under his breath muttered, 'and God help us too'. He'd never seen such a raging sea this side of the sand bar before.

He knew his duty, as had his late father, he must try and save the terrified souls on the stricken yacht, but, as the mighty thud of the maroon shook the night sky and awoke the village, he knew he could be sending men, good men, to their deaths.

Three long, agonising, minutes passed by before crew started to arrive; the first to run in through the now open station doors had more bad news, 'Sid, the mechanic, not coming. . . I saw him. . . He's slipped and done his shoulder. . . B****r, what a night!'

With the odd tweak of their waterproofs to make them comfortable, if that could ever be possible, they gathered at the stern of their stalwart old lifeboat.

'Right lads', shouted the coxswain, 'I don't need to tell you what this storm means to those who are out in it, but I'm not picking the crew tonight; Volunteers only this trip.' To a man they all stepped forward. Old Bob knew they must be afeared, for so was he, only an idiot would have no fear of a cruel raging sea like tonight's. He felt immense pride in his comrades, but this was a time for clear thinking, not emotion.

Old Bob stepped forward and placing a strong hand on one man's shoulder he said 'not you lad, not you ... you stay at station. . . look after everything for our return'.

The man, father of three young boys, was filled with guilt that he was not to go, but knew the coxswain's word was law, and how happy his wife would be that he had not gone to sea - like any of the crew's families would have been that night; that dreadful night, of all nights.

Six men manned the lifeboat that fateful night and all six doubted that they'd see the morrow's dawn as the aptly named 'Princess Dauntless' ran down the slip just as fast as a big wave came in to meet her.

It was one mighty breath taking crash, every one lurched forward, there'd be a few bruises later if they survived, the wave seemed to swallow the boat whole. The Coxswain gunned the powerful diesel engines. . . He must clear the slip and surrounding rocks before the next wave hit and pushed them back.

They were away. . . but only God knew how they would ever return.

The young family man, spared by old Bob, was joined by four or five others who had braved the storm. A storm which was now occasionally hurling swathes of hand numbing sleet at the village; temperatures were tumbling. The volunteers busied themselves, there would be little sleep that night, wet clothes went to the drying room, floors were mopped, doors closed and VHF radio set on the emergency coast guard channel. Someone put the big kettle on the gas and set some chunky white mugs out on the table. . . extra mugs were lined up for the returning crew.

How long those mugs were to sit there waiting no one could ever tell. . . They were lined up in view of the sea through the upstairs window as if waiting, if mugs had feelings they waited with stoic patience and hope.

While the base crew were warm and safe in a station that was built strong to withstand a storm of the century, the lifeboat crew and their boat were taking a beating from breaking waves as they closed on the sand bar, they were truly in a storm of the century, a cutting wind drove sleet and heavy sea spray into the strained faces of the deck crew as they struggled to see any sign of the stricken yacht or its crew.

'No sign skip, no sign yet', shouted one of the crew above the raucous roar of the sea, the howl of the wind and the racing diesel engines.

Without turning from his task of steering a safe path through the boiling sea the Coxswain replied, 'If she's here, we must be close. . . back on deck. . . and for God's sake hang on!'

Often on a trip out to an incident the crew would have time to reflect on life and chat to each other - not so this time - every breath, every heartbeat, every cell of their bodies were focussed on each and every eventful moment as it came rushing from a darkened nowhere and raced by them, as did the rushing sea, into a more darkening past. The next moment could be their last - they were in the firm grip of a merciless storm.

In the cabin the coxswain's second in command wrestled with compass, charts and clock as he desperately tried to keep track of position. While still too much dark cold sea washed over the decks the coxswain also wrestled, not only with the wheel trying to read the waves, but he wrestled with his conscience. Old Bob felt for the deck hands, and allowed himself a moment to wonder if he'd made the right decision. They were all facing death out there and still no sign of the stricken vessel; had she sunk? Was she even really out there? How much longer could they stand this punishment? How would they communicate - coastguard had confirmed this yacht had no radio.

Then, just as they crested a wave, there, in the trough, there she was, lit up by the powerful search lights from the lifeboat, there she was; About a forty footer, sails tattered and with lines and rigging not only strewn on deck but trailing into the sea; No lights showing, no sign of life, the powerful floods and search lights from '*Princess Dauntless*' scoured every visible inch of the heaving yacht - nothing.

With one eye on the moving sea and the other on the tortured yacht, old Bob came alongside as close as he dared; tough as it was their lifeboat could still be damaged and debris in the water choke her engines; no other boats covered this area and with air-sea rescue helicopters grounded - any rescue was up to them - just a handful of men and their 'dauntless' vessel.

'No sign of life - no response', shouts a crew member through the open cabin door.

'Damn, damn, damn,' thought the coxswain, 'as if it wasn't bad enough'. It was one thing to risk life to save life but here they could risk all to find no one on board. Finding a body in this maelstrom of a sea would be without hope or sense, they would be lost for sure. 'Damn, damn, damn', he thought, and while he fought the sea from the wheel he called most of the crew to the inboard cabin, leaving only the searchlight crew up top.

As they gathered, soaked, tired and battered, the Coxswain, always tenacious to the last, said, 'One last chance lads, one last chance. . . we'll board her, search her, and if no luck we'll head up coast and look for shelter. You know I don't like asking you, but, we need a volunteer, we need someone agile, young and strong.' They all, to a man, turned to look at Dave's son, Jim, no doubt the strongest among them. Jim sensed there was no escape from this, better to volunteer, that's after all what they did; put their lives on the line to protect others from the perils of the sea. 'What's the plan? I'll go,' Jim said, clearly and calmly. A couple of good slaps on the back from the crew and the Coxswain explained, 'Be on the port beam, I'll come alongside her from above as we drop down a trough. . . you'll not have long but you should be able to drop on to her deck. As soon as you've gone I'll pull away and hold off. We'll pick you up the same way but we'll come in beneath the yacht and on our starboard side. We'll watch for you all the time, the sea shall not have you. A couple of you go with him to help safely clear the rail. If it looks impossible. . . well. . .' his voice trailed off, there was nothing left to say really.

As the coxswain began to ease the lifeboat into position, he caught a glimpse of the boarding crew through the port side window, they struggled for balance on the heaving deck and were buffeted by the wind, but he could see they were ready, clipped to their safety lines. At last the right sort of wave came along, fairly clean it was and big, and, like toys moved by a child's hand, he put 'Princess Dauntless' alongside with but a foot between them. He saw Jim launch himself beyond the safety rail and then could see no more, with a deft touch he pulled away from the stricken vessel. There was a thumbs up from the deck crew and he knew Jim had made it. The deck crew watched intently as Jim gamely fought his way to the rear hatch of the listing yacht, twice he disappeared from sight, the tension unbearable, and then they could see his lamp moving about inside the cabin. A breaking wave nearly rolled the yacht right over but she recovered, it seemed like forever, one wave came and then another, breaking more frequently now as they closed on more shallows. There was another glimpse of the brave Jim at the fore cabin and then again, nothing. It seemed a lifetime was passing by and hope was fading, but suddenly Jim was up on deck signalling that the vessel was empty. . . no one on board.

Now they started the struggle to claw him back.

'Jim says it's all clear, and he wants to go home!' came the shout into the coxswain's ears. He took a moment to glance over his shoulder and with a smile shouted back, 'stand to then, and let's go fetch him'.

As Jim found a vantage point on the stricken yacht he breathed a sigh of relief. . . at last he was out in the open air and not in a floating coffin where half the time he didn't know which way was up. He had stumbled and fell the length of the yacht, in places water up to his boots, in places up to his neck, there was no sign of life but he'd looked for a body too; he had groped and floundered in the dark water for anything human but only come up with a number of cushions and clothing. He was glad he was out. . .' now, where's my lift home' he muttered through shivering lips.

The yacht teetered on the crest of a wave, rolled a little then started to drop down, beam on. . . his heart skipped a beat. There in the surrounding darkness, a bright jewel of hope, there she was moving in below. . . beautiful to see : '*Princess Dauntless*', with all deck lights bright and deck crew waving, Jim could see two comrades ready by the safety rail they had prepared. His comrades stood ready to catch him, come what may.

It was looking good, he prepared to jump, but the sea was not finished with him yet, just as Jim committed his body to that leap of faith the crest of the wave had broken, dropping heavily on to the yacht; the yacht listed sharply away from the lifeboat and Jim missed his footing, his desperate fingers clawed at the lifeboat's safety line and his comrades were quickly on him with strong hands to draw him to safety. First he felt their determined power as they began like giants to heave him on board... then he felt the sickening pain as the yacht rolled back and crushed one leg between the boats. The Coxswain heard the scream both in his ears and in his heart; a gap appeared between the boats and Jim's semi conscious body was dragged unceremoniously into the cabin. The coxswain cleared the sinking yacht, called for a bearing for the estuary and fixed his eyes, body and soul on the sea ahead; he must get these lads home. An hour later, they were in the sheltered and calmer waters of the river, on shore they were welcomed by an ambulance's blue lights. The crew did their best first aid but by the look of the leg it was not going to be a comfortable transfer.

'You'll be ok'. . .' see you at the station'. . . 'see you in the pub', came the farewells from the crew.

It was a good few long months before Jim was back in the village, his dad drove him down to the station, but he wanted to walk in unaided. He limped in to the familiar faces of all his comrades, picking up on some trivial banter on the way. . . 'Oy, Jim, when you gonna bring them waterproofs back?'. . . 'All right for some, we have to work for a living'. . . but there, sure enough, on the table was his mug, 'Come on', said the Coxswain, 'let's fill this up with something stronger than tea!' As Jim moved forward to pick up his mug he saw next to it was a little blue box. . .'that's yours', shouted one of the crew. Jim picked it up, carefully he opened the hinged lid, and there nestling on velvet was a Silver medal, he read the words to himself, it simply said 'For Gallantry'.

Tea, banter and a little rum flowed and they celebrated Jim's final return from that little adventure they had shared and endured; they were all back together, comrades all..

'Quiet!' shouted old Bob, the room went suddenly silent... the radio in the corner crackled yet again, ... 'Mayday, mayday mayday. . . this is. . .'

While such men live there'll be no end to this story.

§

Whatever you can do, or dream you can. . . begin it.
Boldness has genius, power and magic in it.
Goethe

The author on Fire and Rescue boat, Wisbech

Suspicion.
A rural Edwardian tale of adversity and courage during hard times.

The hurricane lamp swung wildly from its hook on the beam and the flame flickered desperately as the old Inn door opened to the wild night, hurriedly ushering in the wind battered old mole-catcher, Seth. Seth pushed his body against the door to close and latch it; 'By Gor', he said, 'that be proper windy this night, that be'.

'No moles to be caught tonight then Seth', joked the burly innkeeper pouring a tankard of ale from the big jug. 'If I know ee moles, they'll take advantage of this bad weather and be all over his Lordship's lawn by tea time come morning's night', confided the village's oldest, and only, mole catcher; The wind howled like hunting wolves around the ill-fitting casements and doors as if agreeing in chorus.

Seth shuffled his old boots across the sawdust floor, stopping only to briefly add something he no longer wanted to the bar room spittoon. He sat on his favourite old chair near four men, strangers they be, who, though next the inglenook wood fire, still had their great coats on with collars turned up. Caps, the mark of a working man, covered their heads, and their boots looked the worse for wear. Occasionally a gust of wind forced smoke down the chimney, but, oblivious, the men talked on, intent on their secretive liaison.

Seth's friendly, 'Eeenin to ee gents', was largely ignored, only one man, the larger of the four, though they were all stocky built, grunted back, 'An' yerself squire', then quickly turned his back for the work in hand.

'Ah well,' mused Seth, 'obviously strangers, not local accents, seemed sort of. . . well, not sure really. . . anyway, strangers they be and mean looking ones at that. . . wouldn't want to meet them on a dark night. . . mmm'. Seth supped his ale in a peace of his own making.

Now Old Seth might have been getting long in the tooth but there was nowt wrong with his hearing; some said he could hear moles moving underground - some even said he talked to them; old wives tales mostly - mostly.

Seth didn't catch all that was said, he just caught vague snippets of the conversations; 'gorra get money soon', 'thems kahntin on us back ome', 'take arh chances when we can I say', 'wot abart the rich geezer's big owse darn the road', 'shh, not so lahd.'

William, the big innkeeper came close and lighted a callused and powerful hand on old Seth's shoulder, the hand of a part time village blacksmith, 'Zee ere old Seth, I'm putting ee another fine log on the fire to keep ee warm. Now don't ee ferget that kindness when ee next sees his Lordship's woodsmen'.

'Ar, to be certain, there's always plenty of useful men about at his Lordship's', Seth said loudly so as the four men could not fail to hear. At the same time he spoke to William with his eyes, indicating his distrust of the strangers with a sideways look and an enquiring expression.

Seth went back to the bar with William on the pretext of obtaining more ale, but as they huddled over the bar it was other things on their mind. For some half hour they chewed over what they should do about their suspicions but before they could reach a conclusion the Inn door burst open. Standing in the open doorway and of which he had no intention of closing was one of his Lordship the Earl's gardeners, 'big trouble up at the House, need help quick'. By now he has the attention of everyone in the Inn, including the four strangers who are now all looking straight at the gardener with earnest stares.

'What's up, old chap', asked William peering past the wind flickered lantern.

'Fire, Fire. . . stables on fire. . . horses trapped. . . his Lordship is begging for help to save his horses. . . Can you come?'

'We're on our way old chap, we're on our way', as William threw on his rough old coat he shouted at the strangers, 'I'm zorry lads, but us have got to go, ye'll have to leave the Inn, zorry'.

The men stood quickly in unison: 'Nah worries guv, we're coming wiv yer', shouted back the big fellow. With heavy chairs pushed back as though feathers they were all at the door together and out into the dark night. William grabbed two lanterns and they set off hurriedly on the gravelled mile to the Big House; they could smell the fire and hear the horses' tortured cries of fear as they neared the scene.

It was total chaos at the stables, stone built of two stories, the stalls being on the ground floor and storage above, wooden beams, floors and walls every where; straw and winter hay well alight with ever thickening dark yellow smoke, shouts from the servants, even the kitchen girls were there; not that they could do anything much to help. William, Seth and the strangers found his Lordship by the closed main door to the stables, though beside himself with pain for the impending and horrific death of his beloved horses, he managed to explain, 'Fire, started in the loft, burnt through floor, that end of stables, the end where we usually get in, horses down this end but we can't open doors here. . . only from inside, way through is barred by fallen beams and fire. . . My God, just listen to those poor creatures. What can we do?'

'If it can be done sir, it will be done, ee have my werd on it', William said, with a promise in his voice, and with that the six moved as one to the burning end of the building. There was a small bucket chain from the well in use, but of little or no use, they would never extinguish such flames, the only hope was to get in there and open the doors and save the horses, the barn was already condemned to a fiery hell.

William and the big fellow looked through the door together, much of the fire was still on the upper floors, in front of them, a few feet in, was some smoking, water dampened straw and a mess of fallen beams, some of them huge structural beams of oak.

William turned to the big fellow and said, 'Look ee ere, I can't do this on my own, but I reckons it's clear past this point and I reckons I can open they doors an let they 'orses out. Can you. . . will you. . . help I past yon beams?'

'Carnt on us squire, what we bin through we ain't afraid', pulling their collars higher and wrapping some old sacking around their hands and arms they entered through the doorway to hell.

'Seth', shouted William, 'get ee to the main door, tell his Lordship to be ready for they 'orses, and with that he disappeared choking into the yellow grey smoke.

Seth glanced in horror as five men disappeared from sight as though they never were, he hoped upon hope that the building would stand long enough for William to do his work, he then quick as old bones would let him went to find his Lordship.

Strong as William was the beam that barred his way was beyond his moving, as he crouched low to gain some fresher breath, he heard the big fellow shout, ' go fer it mate, we carnt old it up much longah'. William saw through tear blinded stinging eyes the four strangers had lifted the beam enough for him to crawl through. He didn't waste a second, for with every second he was getting weaker and more confused. It was cleaner air further down the stables, he followed the stall fronts on the left to the doorway and, fumbling with shaking but powerful hands, he found the bolts and locking bar that freed the door to open; an almighty shove and fresh air rushed in to greet him as the great door swung open.

As good as his word Seth was prepared, along with the stable boys and his Lordship, to guide the frenzied horses to safety. It was going well, despite the horses being wild and kicking out they were all released safe to a corner field. 'Let it burn now, let it burn,' called his Lordship, 'don't risk yourselves any more, my beautiful horses are safe, God bless you all for your help.'

His composure regained, his Lordship ordered the kitchen staff to prepare refreshments for his helpers, and for everyone to stand back from the now collapsing building; the roof caved in first and carried the first floor down with it, the falling twisting beams levered the stone walls as they fell, it was all but over for the stables.

It was a smoke and sweat smelly throng in the great kitchen, his Lordship mingled with his servants come saviours like they were bosom friends, the like of which was never seen before nor since. 'William, Seth, good friends that you are, heroes both that you are, you will know my gratitude in the days to come, you can be sure of that', beamed his Lordship, who had been as liberal with the port as much as with his thanks.

Seth drew his Lordship aside, 'what of they four strangers, m'Lord, I'm not been seeing they since the fire, perhaps theyms need a watching sir'.

'Nay Seth, good men all, they saved the day for us with their strength and camaraderie, without their bravery our noble William could not have prevailed against the odds as he did. Good men all, simple working folk, iron ore miners walking their way to Northamptonshire for the promise of work to feed their families. I've had the butler sort them out some fresh clothes. . . not burnt ones, eh? Here they come now. Here lads, here, come join us for a meal,' he called.

They sat about the kitchen's great pine table, food and drink a plenty, there they sat, his Lordship, the Mole-catcher, the black-smith and. . . no, not four strangers any more, just four good men that could look any other in the eye and tell their tale.

But I doubt they would, so I have done it for them.

Destiny comes not through chance but by choice.
You are your own destiny.

The Fog.

A mountain rescue somewhere in the Scottish
mountains,one foggy December night.

Inside the loch-side village hall all was bright and warm yet,
outside, it was like another world, a world of darkness, chill
and fog, thick fog.

Inside, laughter and shouting filled the air; the buffet table
was weighted down; it was a special night that night; special
for one man. Tonight they were celebrating the retirement of
old Tam McInnes, thirty years he'd served the mountain rescue, and served with distinction too, but it was time for
younger hands to grasp the nettle. His popularity was evident by the numbers that filled the hall; many others were
simply prevented from being there by an impenetrable fog
that shrouded the group of small mountains and valleys
north of Glen Katrine

Around the hall small groups stood with drinks in hands,
reminiscing, prophesying, or even both. Drinks were drunk
and stories told, some funny some sad. In a small group by
the door one pretty young girl engaged her audience, and
embarrassed her boy friend, himself a prospective candidate
to join the team, by telling how they'd been out walking and
he'd decided to show off his climbing skills instead of going
through a nearby field gate. He'd negotiated the stone wall
all right but sadly for him not the cattle trough the other side.
There was much laughing and slapping of his back. Though
she'd been sworn to secrecy that too, was something that had
conveniently slipped her mind, along with the number of
vodkas she'd had.

At the far end of the hall there was a different mood; new members of the team were listening to Big Jimmy, the long serving village bobby; 'aye,' he said solemnly, 'I've witnessed many an incident come to an end, both good and bad, and it's many a widow and orphan I've had to tell. That's why you boys must do your duty and save the sorrow.' He knew he'd oft times made his 'white lies' as he knocked their doors. . . 'it was all over very quickly. . . he wouldn't have known what was happening. . . he didn't feel a thing.' But he knew the end had oft been fearful and seemingly, endlessly merciless, that pain and despair were their abiding companions as they waited. . . even hoped for death. . . nay, not good, not good. 'We'll be counting on yees t' save they lost souls and bring 'em back safe and sound, we'll be counting on yees.' He stopped abruptly and turned away from their gaze, saying he was off for another sandwich, but in truth he simply didn't want them to see the tear in his eye. . . it just wasn't done you know.

To the skirl of the pipes and a rousing rendition of 'Flower of Scotland' by all present, Tam was lead to the small stage at the far end of the hall. There the local president of the Mountain Rescue Association waited long for the applause, whistling and cheering to subside. He had many a tale to tell of Tam's exploits; some of them told him in whispers of embarrassing moments, some of bloody-minded heroism. Speeches were often boring but this one was going to be good; this was a great night for someone special.

The president had hardly started when his next breath was interrupted by the hall doorway opening and admitting both fog and a shawled lady looking for her son. 'The polis have phoned laddie,' she said, 'there's a farmer missing over yon Ben'.

There was a steady murmur throughout and the president had his chance to at least say something of use. 'All those on call please to the hall doorway to sort yourselves out, the rest of us down this end and keep it quiet please'.

Silence came quick, as it does to those who know its value.

There appeared to be some concerned discussion going on with the team members of the mountain rescue, and retired or not, old Tam McInnes wasn't going to keep his nose out. To gather a full team was going to take a desperately long time due to the dense encroaching fog; also there was snow and bitter weather on the tops so speed was essential. The lost farmer, known by many of the team, and now known as 'the casualty' to depersonalise the issue, farmed beyond the hills above the village. His farm could be accessed by road around the mountains but it was a long way around - too long for comfort.

Tam interrupted the group, who listened intently to a man they had grown to respect immensely over the years, 'I suggest that you make up a small team out of whoever lives in the village itself, take the Landrover from base as far as the track up the valley will allow and make your way on foot to the casualty's last known position. As time permits the rest of the volunteers can take what transport they can and travel by road. I know it'll be a long journey for them, but it seems best to me. What say you?' The murmur of agreement confirmed the plan. 'So, how many of you can be ready in a few minutes from the village?' Tam asked. Six hands went up. Tam surveyed the expectant faces, 'Christine, you lead the team, you know the valley well enough, even in this soup; Robert, go to base and prepare the Landrover and gear for them, don't forget the radios and spare lamps and you can pick up the rest of the team on your way back through the village'.

No sooner was it said than they were gone; gone into an eerie fog-hushed unknown.

As planned, each volunteer, dressed for the terrain and the weather, complete with rucksack of equipment and provisions, was collected by the team's Landrover in the main street. 'All aboard that's coming aboard', called Bob selecting four wheel drive and low ratio.

'Can't you find some more gears in this thing Bob, I've got somewhere to go next weekend!' said a nameless voice from the back. The Landrover crawled out of the village and along the old farm track towards the valley head. They knew Bob was doing his best but it was in their nature to temper the seriousness of their task with the deft touch of highland humour, 'Come on Bob, any slower and we might as well get out and walk'. Bob said nothing and the Landrover staggered on in the sightless mist, lurching from pothole to pothole.

'Here you are you ungrateful lot, this is as far as I can take you. Now hurry up and get out as I've still a pint and dram waiting for me. Have fun', laughed Bob.

'The way you drive Bob we'll be back before you; aye, and with the casualty too', continued Bob's antagonist.

Soon through the field gate and steadily onward they heard the sound of the departing vehicle disappear into the all pervading and stifling mist. Then the only sound was a little heavy breathing as the track turned steeply upward and the steady crump of boots on moving stones. No one spoke, the leader led and the led followed.

Unusually for mountain rescue this group was being led by a woman, Chris by name, a lion hearted little woman of great strength and much experience. She'd lived and worked in the surrounding valley and hills for more years than she cared to tell. Though she knew the terrain like the back of her hand she knew also that this fog was going to test her; the team however, implicitly trusted her judgement.

The five climbed a stile over stone wall, their boots landing softly on grass and heather the other side. All was eerily quiet as the fog deadened all sound, all except the sound of breathing and the light swish of waterproofs.

'Mind your step - small ditch here to cross,' she called back. Each team member repeated the message to the one behind. A soggy squelching sound of boot into boggy ground accompanied by the mumbling of a curse, brought a smile and light chuckle to all but the last team member who was now enthused with gratitude for his gaiters.

An hour into their climb and they were leaving behind all trace of pathways and landmarks, Chris stopped the team, 'take a breather, I'm going to set the compass, let's have another lamp here please'.

Chris had a choice of routes; one, a long way around and following the contours, or, a shorter more direct way that wasn't without the risk and challenge of one or two short climbs. Chris allowed herself a moment to consider what Tam would have done. 'Damn it', she thought, 'I'm not Tam, it's down to me now, must follow my own intuition.' Chris called the team to the map, it was important that everyone knew the plan, 'we're going this way ... it'll save us an hour'. No one questioned her decision; trust was a byword in the survival business.

'I'm all for that,' said Dave, mostly known as 'smiley' by his pals, and now sporting one bog-stained leg, 'Bob must be halfway back to his beer by now. . . I'm looking forward to beating him to it.' Despite their situation, their fog soaked clothes and dewed eye brows; the team gave a little cheer - then just as quickly were quiet again.

'Come on team', urged Chris, 'we're on our own in all this, no helicopter flying and any other teams will be many hours behind us'. Chris had never seen fog as bad, almost as if the Gods had sent it to mark Tam's retirement; one thing for sure it would enter the realm of myths and legends in the village.

They must first cross a stretch of featureless heather moor and Chris sent smiley off in front on her compass bearing. Before losing sight of him the rest of the team would follow, to repeat the process time and again. Slow it may be, but better safe than sorry as the route they were taking had some severe slopes ahead and they must arrive in the right place to avoid them.

'Spot on Chris', shouted back Smiley as he reached a flat and spacious ledge that separated the upper and lower slope.

A sense of excitement ran through the team, the elation of carrying out a perfect navigation on such a night gave them all a feeling of power and achievement. . . but the night was not yet over. In such a small team each and every one of them was essential, one fails, the team fails, tonight they must not fail for they, a mere handful of volunteers, could be all that held the line between life and death for the lost farmer.

Now standing on wet snow the team gathered around Chris and a deft hand wiped clean the misted map case; from their right hand side they could hear the faint sound of falling water. The nearby falls plummet some hundred and eighty feet and when the snows melt are truly magnificent, but tonight the fog concealed its beauty. . . misty spray frozen in space and magical ice structures shaped by nature's artist festooned the ravine side Rowans; it was all out there in the fog and the night - but not for them to see.

Chris pointed to the route on the map, 'up this slope, mostly steep but with peat and heather then we meet the rocky ridge rising up to our left. . . no doubt covered in the same snow as we have here; keep close when we reach the ridge we must find the easiest way through.' The soft slope was steeper than they would have liked, the sort of slope that is easier to go up than down, and this one wasn't easy going up, many a time boots were kicked in to soft ground for a toe hold and hands grabbed lumps of heather for support. As they climbed, each of them living out their own struggle, the air became colder; the fog was beginning to freeze and the ground was hardening as they reached the snow clad rocks of the ridge. Chris and three others made it to the top edge of the ridge, but where was Smiley? In fact he wasn't far away, only a few feet below them, he'd taken a slightly different way but hearing the teams voices so close had believed he was in their footsteps; and he wasn't, he'd gone up a narrow but steep snow clad gully and was now faced with a large smooth boulder, chest height that barred his way; Rock each side of him was like that in front, all worn smooth by centuries, his only foothold just under the base of the obstructing rock so that his body was being pushed backwards. Smiley knew he was in a dangerous spot as he fearfully scrabbled for a good hand hold, but the time worn rock denied him; if he slipped he would be unable to stop himself sliding back down the slope to an even bigger drop beneath.

A concerned voice broke the silence, 'Come on Smiley, what you doing, having a leak?' called one of his mates from above.

'Just coming, nearly there,' Smiley called back hiding his fear in his words and the fog.

Some how Smiley's elbow had found something to push on and in doing so he was able to raise himself up enough to put his body weight over and not under the rock, as it had been since he first became frozen by circumstance. Smiley's legs were shaking a bit as he joined the team, 'OK, made it,' he said putting on a false tone of comfort, 'how the hell did you all get past that snow gully rock - I'm taller than all you, and I struggled; well a little bit, anyway.'

'What rock?' they said in unison, 'we came this way,' so pointing towards a simple open climb.

'Oh,' murmured Smiley, and said no more - but thought a lot!

'OK, team, said Chris, drawing them together again to look at the map, 'we follow the ridge to the summit then drop down the slope on the other side, picking up the stone wall about here', pointing to her chosen start point for the search, 'we'll follow the wall north west and back towards the farm and see what we can find on the way'. She turned to Smiley, now you are nearly back to normal, get on the radio, and give them our current position and status. . . no need to tell them about your ditch or your rock.'

Even Smiley had to laugh, nothing got by Chris. That's why they followed her.

As the fog froze to their eyebrows and their boots made a unified crunching sound on the crisp snow they descended from the ridge summit. 'Message sent Chris, reply is that they are only just getting a back-up team together with transport now,' said Smiley having jogged quickly by the others to be at Chris' side. It was a good half mile to the wall, they were aiming high so as to be sure of picking up the gateway shown on the map on the way down, no need to use the technique they used earlier, this was all open sheep grazing land in the summer. Boot prints in the snow disappearing into a dark and claustrophobic past showed that they were keeping a good line.

'Wheesht! Listen. . . all quiet!' commanded Chris.

They all stood silent, their lamps creating reluctant rays of light into the all pervading fog, they could all hear it .... no doubt about it ... the sound of an idling diesel engine .... 'sounds like we've found someone's Landrover,' said Smiley quietly. Mountain rescue never counted their chickens before they hatched, they never knew what they would find but all the while must keep enough strength to make it home again - never easy.

'This way', called Chris, 'we'll head straight for it and if abandoned we'll look for tracks. Wait till we get there before radioing in a message - let's see what we've got first.' Their pace and hearts quickened to the task and it was not long before the shape of a Landrover tilted over to one corner loomed out of the mist, like a whale from the deep.

The side lights and cab light were on and there behind the wheel looking right as rain sat George the farmer. He'd had a fright earlier when trying to return home; he'd lost a wheel into a dip near the wall, then trying to extricate it had twisted his ankle. He'd liberally used hill farmer language to bewail his predicament - not that it was going to help him, and he'd resigned himself to a long wait till morning.

Well, the fright he'd had earlier was to pale into insignificance compared with the almost heart stopping fright he had as his tediously unchanging view through misted up windows suddenly filled with lights; and strange faces with only their eyes visible. What a relief it was as he heard a familiar voice, 'what are you doing sleeping out here George, your wife wants you back home.'

'By jings it's you lassie, you gave me a fright Chris, I thought they'd come for me at last,' George smiled.

'So George, what is your situation, can you walk?' asked Chris through the now open door. George explained in hill farmer terms that if he could walk he'd already be home in front of his dinner by now. Chris was pleased they'd found the old boy alive and reasonably well, 'Smiley, get on the radio and tell them back at base, 'casualty located, minor injuries, team and casualty making its way to Low Ben Farm, will contact by landline on arrival, ETA approximately thirty minutes.'

'Now George, you're a bit of a lump for us few to carry you down to the farm. We'll have to *drag* you down,' Chris said with a wry smile, just visible to George through the fog. A quick glance in the back of the Landrover revealed the makings of a sledge of sorts; using the team's fold up stretcher and some canvas sheeting the team soon had it made and had George well wrapped up with almost anything to spare and the odd 'space blanket' thrown in. With four corners of the canvas gripped by a team member each and Chris leading the way. Not without frequent advice from George - it has to be said - the sledge made easy going over the hardened snow.

With George's encouragement, for he'd not eaten in a while, and advice given on the best way down the fields, they were knocking on the farm door in just over twenty minutes. After the initial shock it was a merry welcome to all the team; and a sharp word to her daft old husband too; outdoor clothes off and warming in the back scullery while a phone call was made to stand down all other teams and soon hot plates full of egg, bacon and chips weighed down the farmhouse table. No need to rush back. . . nothing to rush back for.

Lizzie, George's wife, poured the tea and thanked the team. 'Tonight', she said 'is a night for one special person, and with a tear of joy in her eye turned to Chris and said, 'May God bless you for bringing my man back from the hills. Only someone special could have done this thing. Thank you Chris.'

There was a loud cheer from the team and the clink of a bottle as George - unusually voluntarily - dug out his best whisky. There was no rush anymore.

Beyond the hills, way down by the loch, they still celebrated the retirement of their honoured guest, Tam, once mountain rescue leader.

In a wee fog bound highland farmhouse somewhere in the mountains they celebrated the birth of a new one.

Faith is the bird that feels the light when the dawn is still dark.
Unknown

Cautionary

Scrooge?
Poor old boy.

'Ah, Christmas is coming', they said.

'Mmm, I don't like Christmas', he replied, but inwardly reflecting that it perhaps wasn't Christmas itself, but how he felt about it and its associated little tragedies.

'Bah, humbug. You Scrooge! Came a quick, accusing chant, and not without a hint of opinionated bitterness, from the two Christmas lovers, a trait that was absent in his own view on Christmas, it has to be said.

'Ah, poor old Scrooge, how maligned the poor old boy has been portrayed'. He said, quietly.

'Rubbish! He was just a mean old man that hated Christmas', they replied.

Turning to them, he said, 'Was he really? What do we know of his suffering, his feelings, and his endeavours; just because Dickens chose, for his own twisted purpose, not to write about them in his book? People only loved Scrooge once he gave them what they wanted. . . his money, like spoiled children when they didn't get what they wanted the 'I hate you' syndrome kicked in'.

Warming to a task they relished each year they retorted, 'What about poor old Bob Cratchit then, trying to feed his family on low wages, and having to work at Christmas?'

'So, Scrooge, who was not the father of any of Cratchit's proliferate children, must provide for a man who hasn't planned to live within his means? How many of us would be pleased to so do? And in those dark days of servitude and hunger, was not Cratchit gainfully employed and paid a fair wage - if he was that good and could have earned more and done better then surely he would have changed jobs?'

'Pah, Scrooge was doing alright for himself and should have. . . er. . . should have er. . . helped others and joined in at Christmas,' they blurted.

('Oy,' they complained to the writer, 'you're writing us in a bad way. . . not giving us a chance'.

'My point exactly,' thought the writer.)

'Look, Cratchit ate better than Scrooge; Scrooge often ate warmed up gruel for his meal, Cratchit would have soon complained if that's what he got. . . and so would you too. Scrooge was no hypocrite either, he could have gone every year to his nephew's for a free slap up Christmas dinner, but did he? No, he didn't, true to his values and beliefs his dinner was to be the cheap gruel he usually had, while Cratchit with his whole family had eyes on the butchers for a big turkey that they couldn't afford. In years to come Scrooge's lack of reckless investment and borrowing beyond his means, coupled with his ecologically friendly frugal use of fossil fuels and to live with what we need and not with 'what we want', will be held up as a shining example of humanity and not the pariah as you choose to see him. Scrooge took little for himself, while all around him as Christmas approached, thousands of living trees were to be hacked down, once dead to be discarded, thousands of animals slaughtered to lie half eaten in the bins of merry makers, people sent greetings to those they could hardly remember and looked forward in misery to a compulsory meal with family members they often couldn't stand'.

His listeners sighed exasperatedly. He continued, 'and another thing, Scrooge was a leader; it was only through the drive and endeavour of Scrooge that Cratchit even had employment. Not only this, but reading between the lines of Dickens' character assassination, Scrooge at no time asked Cratchit to do anything he would not do himself - now that is truly a rare man, remember, he was already at work in the cold when Cratchit rolled in late for work; yes, a leader indeed. He didn't have a wardrobe full of Victorian designer clothes, no plush furniture, no servants, and no grand pictures on the wall; he lived a simple life in which he condemned no other - unlike what was to become of him from the mind and pen of Dickens'.

'You old humbug you', they said in unison, 'Where's your Christmas spirit?'

'Mmm, Christmas spirit eh? Well at least you won't be plagued with the spirits that visited Scrooge, poor man, no doubt yours are likely to be Baileys and Advocat, and in some excess to boot, meanwhile let us be in good spirit for whatever life we lead. With eyes and minds only on the 'material' of this Earth we might miss out on the 'spiritual', and if not careful will have less time than was given to Scrooge to put it right. Scrooge was surely inherently a good man all his life, it was only when he started his 'handout' spree that others 'saw' it for the first time. Or did they see what they thought they saw? If Dickens was to truly espouse the Christmas spirit he would have written in a refusal for payment by the boy sent to the butchers; the child could have said, 'keep your shilling sir, for on this Christmas day I'll gladly help you for free'. But he didn't, did he? And what of that giant Turkey? Did Dickens write in an honest comment from Mrs Cratchit, mmm, I doubt it, more like it went, 'we'll never cook this blooming thing in time for dinner, and it won't go in the oven, what burke bought this?' One of the children probably said 'I'm sick of turkey, why can't we have some gruel instead'.

You see, Dickens only wrote what he wanted you to know, perhaps he wrote the story as revenge on an old rich uncle who had denied Dickens as a boy for some frivolous Christmas present he had hankered and whinged over - who knows?

Scrooge eh? Poor old boy.'

Not sure you like this version? Then how do you think Ebenezer felt when that man, Dickens wrote what he did about him in the tabloid of the day? Still don't like it? Then it is simple. . . write your own!

A wise man hears one word but understands two.

Hope; the greatest of all evils?

She lived on the sixth floor of a block of 1960s flats, one of the few drab grey monoliths still standing in the area; a fitting memorial to a long gone and failed social experiment. It was in one of those places where, just like had she, you could live for several years and never even see a neighbour let alone talk to one.

The living room, still with its 1960s wallpaper of nondescript green leaf did not fail to show its age. The room gave access to a tiny balcony via the windows that faced south and enjoyed far reaching views beyond the conurbation to gently rolling farm clad hills and some still surviving ancient woodland. It was a bright and sunny day and with reasonable eyesight one could see, soaring majestically, a lone Buzzard harried by rooks high above the woods. The Buzzard always seemed to be able to rise above the conflict and merely dipped his wings and changed direction to avoid the attack, moving on in unperturbed serenity, borne aloft by nature's generous gifts.

'Hey, come quick and see the birds,' called her friend Solomon, in an excited tone as he watched the buzzard through the open window, 'Wow, that really is beautiful. . . don't miss it. . . come on. . .'

Solomon had been a good friend for many years and, when allowed, an occasional visitor who had always sought to brighten her life somewhat; he seemed an ever hopeful, ever positive warrior in his late thirties, whilst she was an ever negative worrier in her early forties. 'No, can't at the moment, there's a charity advert about children in need. . . poor things they don't stand a chance. . . anyway, Eastenders

Omnibus is on next and I want to watch it again, they kill off one of the heroes next episode. . . I wonder who it will be. . . and you know I can't put the TV in the sunny room as I can't see the picture. . .' she complained from her half bedroom half living room on the North side of the flat; in general mostly cold and often damp around the single glazed window that over looked the backs of shops and a derelict factory unit; black mildew lived undisturbed and contentedly behind her mother's old wardrobe.

'I know', replied Solomon brightly, 'let's go out for a walk to the park. . . feed the ducks, see the squirrels or something . . . It'll be fun, come on.'

There was a considerable pause before her reply, as the advert wasn't quite finished, 'No, I don't want to, it will be dark soon and I'm not paying good money for bread just to throw it away on some old ducks that should be able to care for themselves.'

Solomon's exploring eyes were drawn to some children far below, boys and girls, playing football on the little council green between the car parks; it looked like great fun, he could sense their laughter and high spirits. . .'There are some children playing on the green, let's go and watch. . . perhaps get to join in if we're lucky.'

There was another long pause as he heard the theme tune to her programme finishing. . . 'certainly not, horrid kids, their parents should keep them indoors. . . I bet it's them doing all that graffiti too.'

'OK,' sighed the ever hopeful Solomon, now coming more to the real purpose of this visit. He brightened his voice again and, while reaching into his jacket pocket to reassuringly touch his as yet undelivered bundle of love letters, continued, 'I have an idea, let me take you out for a meal, then we'll go to the cinema; I hear there's a great film on at the new Multi-screen, all about a young woman who finally meets the man of her dreams but then struggles to find a way to tell him. . . it's supposed to be very funny. . . What do you say?'

'No, I'm not interested in a daft film about some stupid woman chasing an even more stupid bloke. . . doesn't appeal to me at all. I've got some dinner in the fridge anyway; you go out to eat if you like. . . I don't think there's enough for two as it is. . . it's a mix of various things that I've had leftover during the week. It's all go that flippin' cooking lark, all go I tell you. I'm a slave to my kitchen, always stuck in, that's me.'

Always keen to please her, 'How about I get a Chinese take away, freshly cooked, very tasty, that would be nice, my treat, and I'll fetch it too,' offered Solomon, his friendly voice again reaching out to her.

'No, don't like Chinese food, never liked it since I over-heard someone in a post office queue. . . and what a damn long one it was too. . . they should have more counter staff I say. . . anyway they said that they knew of a neighbour's friend who knew someone who'd holidayed in Krasnaker-stanovia where they'd eaten a Chinese meal and it made them all ill.'

'Now there's an idea', said Solomon with far off dreaming eyes gazing to the left and, along with his soul, drawn towards the setting Sun; a beautiful sky that glowed yellow through orange to the prettiest red that he'd ever seen; 'Why don't we go on a nice holiday together, it would do you good to get out and I've not had a holiday for years now, what with the pressure of my charity work on top of full time hospital duties. Yes, that would be wonderful; what do you say? What about a cruise? I'll help with money if that's a problem.'

'No, I'd be sea sick for a start, never was any good at trav-elling, I haven't really done any since I remember my mum saying I was sick on a bus when I was two or three. No, you go if you like; I have every thing I need here.'

The theme tune played itself out to the bitter end and she slowly got up and pushed her feet into some tatty and cheap slippers and stubbed out her cigarette before it went too far down the filter. Pulling an old dark cardigan tighter around her shoulders she walked through to the sunny living room. Very unlike him, Solomon had already gone. She half wondered, half hoped that he may have gone to fetch that take-away, she was quite hungry now and that rubbish in the fridge was really destined for a bin of the same name. As the Sun set lower she closed the window and drew the curtains against the setting Sun and impending cold of evening; she flicked the switch on her coal effect electric fire and she waited for the phone or the doorbell to ring. Solomon was truly such a fine chap, such good company; she missed him now he was gone and she sat and waited for his return.

The doorbell rang and she quickly rose to her feet, she'd been thinking about the cinema again and the holiday too, how great it would be to share Solomon's wisdom and happy company on such an adventure of a lifetime. Quickly she tidied the cushions and excitedly walked to the door, a spring in her step, pausing only to adjust her clothes and hair in the mirror.

She opened the door with a bright smile that soon disappeared, as quick as had Solomon, when she saw two uniformed constables standing in the dim light of the concrete hallway.

They could see she was shocked and the first said calmly, 'may we come in Ma'am; we have some questions we'd like to ask you. . . best you take a seat first. . .'

She sat down, perched on the edge of her two seat settee and clutching at her cardigan with both hands, 'Oh, dear, Oh, dear, what is it, why are you here? She implored.

The first began again in a compassionate but official manner, 'It's about a gentleman by the name of Solomon Ma'am, we have some bad news, I'm afraid that there's no easy way Ma'am, it looks very much like suicide, if it's any consolation ma'am it would have been over very quickly, he couldn't have suffered.'

Shocked and totally surprised by such news as she could never ever have expected, she wondered why the officers knew to come to her door. . . 'but how did you know. . ?' The second officer completed her sentence for her, 'how did we know to come here? Well, the location of the body below those windows Ma'am and we also found a bundle of seemingly yet-to-be delivered letters in his pocket with your name and address, that's how we found you so quickly. I know this is difficult Ma'am but we have to ask. Do you know any reason at all that could help with enquiries as to why he would jump to his death. . . anything at all ma'am that could help us close the case, Ma'am'.

Her hands wrung at her cardigan, dear Solomon, gone. . . 'Oh, no, officer , none at all. . . why, he was the most kindly, gentle soul, so full of life, full of hopes and dreams, always happy, positive, he loved nature, travel, good food. . . he loved life itself. . . in fact I never knew anyone with so much to live for. . . I'm so sorry I cannot help you more, that's really all I ever knew of him. . . poor lovely Solomon.'

'Thank you for your patience Ma'am, we'll let ourselves out, sorry about the bad news Ma'am.' As they stood in the doorway before closing the door, the second officer spoke kindly, 'we can't let you have the letters yet Ma'am. . . must go to the coroner first. . . When that's all over I'm sure they will be forwarded to you. . . I'm sure that's what he would have wanted all the time'

The door closed quietly but firmly on one sad lady, in the background the theme tune began for Coronation Street; she sat motionless, lost in thought, clutching at her cardigan.

Nietzsche, the German philosopher once said,
'Hope is the greatest of all evils, for it prolongs the torment of man'

However, 'To smile or cry is forever our own choice.'

The Writing Competition.

Once upon a time a despairingly overlooked author fidgeted nervously on the psychiatrist's couch; eaten up with angst, he was encouraged to examine and confront his burgeoning mental suffering - but not as much as was being suffered in the drawing room of a grand old Georgian house on the other side of town. . .

The self elected senior judge critically browsed the entries, none as good as his own of course. 'Here; just look at this one,' he said, slapping the paper onto the table, stubbing heavily thrice, with anything but a writer's finger, at the text.

Two curious and subservient junior judges obligingly scanned the pages;

'Mmm,' mused the plump one, 'very novel idea for a story, though I detect objectionable undertones. No! I don't like it; it's too, sort of, personal, almost offensive.'

Obscuring his pretentiousness, the thin judge interceded, 'we mustn't, just on a whim, throw out fair play and the accepted rules on judging'; at the same time he thought that 'plump' had been a kindly euphemism. The senior judge peered over his spectacles sternly, cautioning as to the dangers of ignoring a story's literary merit, otherwise judges could be accused of personal bias. 'As if, eh?' thought the plump one. The senior continued, 'There seems to be something odd about the writer, almost deranged, if not, at least deluded. I mean, he could be dangerous'.

The plump one, full of courage, profiteroles, and Baileys too no doubt, dismissed offhand any dangers. 'Well, I've never seen headlines, 'Competition judges assassinated by lunatic author', she laughed contemptuously.

The thin judge nervously scratched his groin with one hand and picked up his copy of the story with the other; the plump judge shuddered in disgust and picked up hers.

One silence imperceptibly followed another; their minds transfixed on disposing of this entry to the bin – while still keeping their kneecaps intact.

There was a tentative tapping at the door; they twitched as though caught doing something naughty. The senior demanded, 'Who's there?'

'It's me love, I've brought you some tea and home made cakes; shall I bring them in?' It was his seemingly never to please him wife. In chorus they shouted, 'Bring it in.'

In she came, wooden tray laden with the best china tea set and lovely home baked cakes.

The papers were thoughtlessly brushed aside, tumbling unnoticed into the waste bin.

'More tea?'. . . 'Yes please'. . . 'Another chocolate brownie?' . . . 'Mm lovely'. . .

They soon forgot that awful story that they must, at some later date, still judge; fate will decide but, now, it was cake and tea time!

'Well, yum, yum, yum', said the senior judge with an unlike him at all expression

'Scrummy, just scrummy', said the plump one, forcing the last cake into her left cheek, the right still occupied by an earlier one.

'My goodness, your wife's a good cook', exclaimed the thin judge, as he carefully brushed nonexistent crumbs off his groin.

' Oh no', said the little woman, 'please, no credit to me, a nice young man, so polite, though a trifle strange, brought them to our door not more than an hour ago – 'a little surprise', he'd smiled. . . 'for the competition judges'.

'Publish or be damned'

It was all image but with little substance; a notable address, posh façade, large glossy red front door and big, polished brass letter box, but they were to obscure from everyone, except the lone business tenant, a dingy rabbit warren of musty rooms.

It was to this seemingly prestigious address, Buckingham Manor, Bishop's Road, those adventuring packets, nurturing treasured dreams and aspirations, would steadily be delivered.

Brown paper packets no doubt lovingly bound and sealed with a prayer and perhaps a kiss, trembling hands to almost reluctantly but yet excitedly pass this treasure into the hands of the local postmaster; then to go home and wait; and wait; like an enfant perdu.

'Clonk, thunk'. The little brown paper parcel leaves the letter box and hits the un-carpeted floor of *Mirage Publishers; publishers of Repute '*.

After a short while, a heavy footed, stern faced but well dressed woman clumped her way to the door, picked up the parcel and some bills with a dismissive, 'Humph', and returned along the dim hallway to her office, the nerve centre of her cold business world. The ground floor office had a single window of Victorian sash; it was the only clean window in the building and overlooked an overgrown and unkempt rear garden. She brushed aside some sweet wrappers and cigarette ash with a piece of glossy advertising material; '(*Mirage Publishers*, generously offers hope to writers of all genres; 3 easy steps to seeing your life's work in quality print; you are not alone, our established and talented team of advisers are always on hand to assist. . . etc.)'

'Mmm', she thought, 'good advert that, things have picked up since I used the tabloids to access the hopeful and the hopeless'.

Without a glance at the return address she scrummaged the defenceless brown paper off the book inside and binned it, though it did not stay there long for it creaked it's way open again and toppled off the heaped bin on to an ornate Persian rug, for which, though purchased in a charity shop, she had still aggressively bargained; it was warm under her feet and a constant reminder of her long and privately held motto.

She stared out of her only clean window on the world outside, peering into the overgrown jungle it had become; she sipped grandly on a drop of East European Scotch Malt and wondered what, if anything, was living out there.

Eventually her eyes and mind returned to the moment and she picked up the book and opened the cover, there was the draft title, '*Publish or be Damned*'. Her mind toyed with the idea, was it 'interesting', or plain 'spooky'? She settled for it being a misprint and read 'and' for 'or', besides the idiot author hadn't even included their name!

She turned the page; '*Dedicated to all those lost souls who never found peace. May this book save and protect all those whose path once began the same*'.

'Aha!' she grinned, 'Another nutter, no doubt', and sipped some more of the Scotch; the bottle had such a grandiose label, with rich colours and a wonderful double headed eagle.

The next page was to startle her more, it read,

'Clonk, thunk'. The little brown paper parcel leaves the letter box and hits the un-carpeted floor of '*Déjà vu Publishers*,'

She read on; it was all about a publisher, the books she receives and what she does with them. She could not put the book down, mesmerised, it was as though she had been absorbed, drawn in. She mused briefly, 'the sign of a good author this', before she again was lost in a world of print and ideas.

The day was darkening and, as if it were someone else's, her hand reached out and clicked on the desk lamp, a sound silent to her deaf ears.

There was something strangely familiar about the story, seemingly as though she may have read it before; most peculiar.

It was as though she were not reading but that the book spoke to her; it spoke to her of how each and every book she had ever received carried innately with it a small piece of the writer's soul; it spoke of how a book contains much of the writer, it arrives on the publisher's floor with more than packaging, it arrives with longing, with fear, with hope, with dreams, with prayers - and not all to God either. The book spoke on in silence, 'until we writers have a reply then our tormented souls are not complete, for part is lost and trapped; far away in an old and dusty mortuary of a back-room office'.

'My God', she thought, 'how intuitive, that's just what I have done'.

She shivered as drawn in deeper still as in a day dream, she was neither conscious of her own body nor could see the print, and the pages may as well have been blank. But still the book spoke on,

'. . .pieces of soul in the musty recesses of the book dump seek each other out to find a strength in unity; When strong enough, they grow into a presence that many a visitor will feel with an unknowing shiver. The tormented soul beast knows no way home, trapped in a dead library of unseen and unvalued books. Books, sent out with a begging tear, never to be opened, their pearls of wisdom, hope, laughter and tragedy doomed never to spill like seeds on to the rich fields of human imagination.'

A pang of guilt echoed through the hollows of her body, and, without sound or feeling she stood and walked through to the 'book store'; there she was surrounded by laughter and sadness, by drama and adventure, by horror and the unknown mystical, she began to pick up books and thumb the dusty pages to see what she might have missed before; the deeper and deeper she delved into the essence the more blindingly obvious it all became.

Some months later, the owner of the old terraced property, in the company of a police constable, pushed open the dirty red door with its grubby brass letter box against a heap of letters, books, and bills.

'There; look,' says the owner. 'Just as I thought, she's cleared off and left all the bills - and me - unpaid, Pah! I tell you'.

They searched the building, expecting nothing and finding nothing, except a single bulb still burning in a back office. The constable switched it off while the owner grumbled, 'I suppose I'll have to pay for that too! Do you know officer; she didn't even leave a name!'

Local auctioneers, Scrimp & Sons, billed as 'expert house clearance specialists', were called in to do their best. The job was handed down to two older men and a young lad, part timers, 'no need for skill on this job', thought old Claude Scrimp.

'The desk and carpet goes for auction', said the foreman, 'any of them books look arf decent box 'em up and take them too. All the rest lob in the skip. Look lively; I want to be home fer tea tonight.'

The young lad picked up a new looking book, fresh printed, by its appearance; 'ere look', he said excitedly, his first time on a clearance, 'this ones never bin opened'. He flicked through the pages and stopped by chance, or so he thought, on a most interesting page. 'Cor blimey, listen ere to this', he calls with glee, 'its all abart some woman who gets trapped in a book and can't get out, 'cos no one ever reads it, blimey, 'ows abart that then?'

The foreman shouted from the open door, 'Bet it's total cobblers; now chuck it in the bin and get on wiv it or you'll be getting all of the top floor stuff next job we get'.

'Clonk, thunk'. The book hit an uncarpeted skip floor.

The young lad looked around, not sure if he'd heard a scream of distress or maybe was it laughter, he couldn't tell. 'Can't be bothering with that,' he thought, 'not with the guvner wanting his tea on time. Priorities, that's the thing yer know, some things are just too important to be messed with.' 'Clonk thunk.' 'Clonk thunk.' 'Clonk thunk'.

The present time is the only time over which we have dominion. The most important person is always the person with whom we are, who is right before us, for who knows if we will have dealings with any other person in the future. The most important pursuit is making that person happy for that alone is the pursuit of life.

Tolstoy

Humorous

Trepidation filled the home
- it was back!

It was a little early to be up, the grey autumn sky resting after a night's rain. He turned on the electric fire and put on some warm clothes and wandered, still only half awake, into the conservatory. He had already given himself instructions on the number of jobs he was to make sure he did that day ... and he felt that 'himself' was going to be a little lazily resistant to the tasks ... now there in front was another one.

There hanging dry but sadly crumpled, as though abandoned, on the old clothes rack were a few items of the more intimate attire. 'Aha', he thought, 'let's clear these away first, it'll make a good start to the day'. So saying to himself, 'himself' started to fold neatly the still crumpled and never to be ironed undergarments, then taking the socks - M&S socks you know, not just any old socks - size 12 to 14 s they were , and they fitted his feet nicely, much better than squeezing them into the size 7 to 11s he'd always had before.

Three pairs of light and dark green socks were folded into each other for protection - so that they could keep guard over each other against the unknown. Then, he looked aghast at the lone sock, a new sock, all alone, its partner gone into the great ethereal home of the 'socknapper'.

He knew it would be a waste of time searching, it had happened before, sometimes the hostage would be returned surreptitiously to be found with total amazement by the owner, usually with the cry, ' how the devil did that get there?'

It had been a recent crime, he looked down at his currently sock-less feet against the terracotta carpet, and counted them, sure enough he still had a pair of them, and not long ago they were adorned and comforted by a pair of fine socks, perhaps never to be seen again.

These were new socks and not long ago could this crime have been committed as he had removed them from his feet only a couple of days previously and placed them in the washing machine, washed them then hung them out to dry . . .Now one of them was alone and possibly never to be reunited with 'himself's' feet. . . A tragedy for a sock that was born into such noble service, perhaps for years now it would lie lonely and unwanted in a dusty drawer , waiting, just waiting and hoping that the sock napper would either return its mate or take it too so they may be together again. . . perhaps to adorn some mystical and unearthly feet in the nether world of the socknapper, no doubt attracted to the house by the scent of brand new socks herding in pairs in the great sock drawer.

Himself wondered, though only very briefly as experience had taught him it was a useless exercise, where the socknapper could possibly live. . . it could not be far away as it was only a few feet from washing machine to dryer. . . now, the socknapper is surely invisible as no one has ever reported seeing one, yet we know they must exist, does it make the borrowed socks invisible too, and they lay all over the house, our human eyes blind to their presence?

Ah well. . . from now on 'himself' must guard his dwindling and valuable sock collection with renewed vigour. . . Until the socknapper has moved on. . .

Perhaps to your house!

later t at day evid nce of a let er napper als began to ap e r. W at nex he wond r d.

> *No argument is so convincing*
> *as the evidence of your own eyes.*

Mr and Mrs Karavana
take a well earned break.
Any other breakages were purely incidental

It was early summer and already some of the nation's schools had broken up for holidays and for once the British weather forecast was unusually optimistic.

It was on a hot and sunny Friday afternoon, having left his Hampshire home a few hours before (*address withheld for security reasons*) that Silas Ebenezer Karavana, Rotarian and retired accountant, trundled his car, his wife Brunhilda Adolfina Karavana, and their posh, state of the art caravan along a charmingly winding and unfettered west country road.

'Oh, look at the lovely views dear', he said leaning forward and to his left to have a look at some steep wooded valley. She slapped her crossword magazine down onto her lap, 'Never you mind the views. . . you just watch where you are going. . . Plenty of time for views when we arrive.' She glared at him over her glasses. Once Silas' satisfactorily admonished eyes were back on the empty road in front she continued in a more conciliatory tone, 'How lucky we are with the roads, you would have thought that people would have wanted to take advantage of such a nice weekend.'

They did. . . oh, indeed they did and, moving so very slowly south westerly, a few hundred of them languished in the exhaust of the Karavana's old under-powered petrol engined Ford, unable to safely overtake the Karavana's latest proud acquisition, a wide frame, 30 foot caravan, which Silas and Brunhilda called 'home' from time to time, the manufacturer's called 'Viking Marauder III', and most motorists called 'that which may not be written'.

Silas couldn't see any of the following hordes mind you, as he had forgotten to fit the wide plastic clip on mirrors, you know, the special ones for humanity-impoverished caravan, horse and boat towers. . . otherwise all they see behind them is their own trailer. Funnily enough they'd remembered a half pint of milk from the fridge, a half bottle of tomato sauce from the cupboard and two urns of dog ashes that they planned to scatter on a nice little tourist beach they knew of, but they were at the end of their street when he'd noticed the missing mirrors. Brunhilda abruptly put his mind at rest, 'You don't need those silly things, and we're not going back now, what would the neighbours think'. Not that they had cared much for their neighbour's thinking while their caravan blotted out the sun and the view as it pressed against their fence for most of the year. Anyway, Silas had heard at the Grubstaker Caravan AGM they only used those mirrors to count cars in hope of entering *The Guinness Book of Records* for longest tailback; currently held by a chap in his eighties who towed a travelling dog kennel with his mobility scooter through the Lake District one Bank Holiday - so rumour had it.

'I suppose you're right yet again dear, after all it's only a few hours drive then we're parked up for a couple of weeks, I don't suppose they'd make any difference', he agreed. 'Compromise is always best,' he thought.

'Dozy clod', she thought back.

As the tedious miles wore on relentlessly, every now and then in a semi-conscious fit of desperation some rabid lunatic would scorch by on the wrong side of the road and disappear in seconds into the distance in a cloud of burning oil, fuel and rubber. 'Absolute nutters,' Brunhilda fumed, 'they should be shot and prosecuted'. And that indeed was the order in which she foresaw the punishment. 'Where are the police when you want them, I say', she continued, having a little mock cough over the diesel particulates left suspended in the still air trapped between the roadside hedges and trees. Meanwhile, at a junction some two miles back, an officer of the law continued to wait for the convoy to pass or someone to let him out. As sure as eggs is eggs this was not going to happen, as most drivers, complete with car crammed with luggage, screaming children, nagging wife, snoring mother-in-law and a dog with head out of window wondering why its cheeks and ears weren't flapping in the breeze, had been in the queue long enough to have been soul numbingly stripped of all humanity and good will.

Some of the trailing drivers were doing OK; there were the Yogis that saw every small delay as a chance to practice breathing meditations and Mudra hand shapes while holding the wheel, and there were those that had something unpleasant waiting at the end of their journey, who, if anything, hoped their journey would never end, or workmen who were counting the overtime payment at every tick of the clock or the dull of wit who were happily listening to a repeat four hour radio show about knitting on St Kilda in the 1600s narrated in Glaswegian American on the World Service.

Those drivers that were most certainly not doing OK were those with business appointments, those with pregnancies on their mind, either concluding one or starting one, those with dinners already cooking in a pre-timed oven, those with travel sick children in competition with the family dog as to who could bring up the most and scoring points for inconvenience. . . like the passenger's lap or the driver's neck, then there were those whose ability to control their bladder was fading with increasing pain and diminishing muscle strength.

Where the hell could they stop, if they ever found a parking spot, they'd never leave it again and if they did stop a thousand laughing or 'must look but be disgusted' faces would be watching them as the doomed cavalcade droned on by.

It was some of they that took life, opportunity and bladder in hands as they squinted already glazed eyes westwards into the blindingly bright setting Sun, changed down a couple of gears and prayed that they would be met around the bend with an empty road and not a herd of sheep or tractor as they gunned their engines in a panic that befitted those about to die of an imminent ruptured bladder.

Further back down the winding road, behind the oblivious and content Karavanas, was a trail of debris and destruction, both material and human. There were poor drivers who couldn't afford a service, nor the AA either, half parked on a scrap of grass verge with steam issuing from radiator and ears alike. . . just a little more speed would have cooled their engine. . . just a tiny bit more. . . not much to ask from life. There were sporadic minor bumps as distraught and distracted drivers nudged the car in front, driven by someone in a similar state. Luckily the only deaths were to insurance no claim bonuses. 'Can we keep the police out of this mate, I just can't take any more points on the licence, damn this awful road, what on earth is causing the jam. . . I bet when we get there there'll be nothing in sight.'

Three cars back a budding and promising holiday relationship was ending abruptly and prematurely and five cars back a surprise divorce was being worked out. Ten cars back and the bloke was making plans to have the family dog re-homed when the holiday was finished. . . unless it drowned at sea or something similarly fortuitous before then. Anxieties over the little pointy thing that told them fuel was nearly all gone triggered angina and migraines among more of the unlucky wretches that day .... 'I told you to get petrol at the supermarket, but you wouldn't listen, would you .... Oh no, you always know best, don't you. . . now look at the state we're in. . . I'm not pushing this car again. . . you did the same in 1962 when we were courting. . . my mum said you weren't that bright then either, don't know why I married you. . . now I need a wee.'

Picking up on the same thought Silas had bought himself a little unit advertised in 'Non Stop Caravanning For Middle Englanders'. It was a bargain, only £29.95, with chain attached screw top bung and made of recycled plastic in camouflage green. Although they had a loo in the caravan the Karavanas much preferred to use other people's and in any event when Silas had stopped in the past he'd been most annoyed to find that the empty road he once enjoyed had suddenly become busy. . . and no one would ever let him back into the traffic, 'miserable wretches,' he'd thought, 'have they no soul?'

Well it wouldn't happen now, not with this new equipment, 'Excuse me my lovely, would you pass me the Wallmart 'Weelief' unit please dear', he asked nicely as he slowed the vehicle to fiddle with his trouser zip. Although Brunhilda found the process somewhat lower class she realised that it was more prudent for their slow-towed vehicle to remain mobile and not leave the road; she herself abstained from drinking for twelve hours before a drive but old dozy had finished off a carton of sell-by-date-reduced orange juice at the house. A quick change down a gear to relieve the again struggling engine and Silas urinated satisfyingly at about thirty miles per hour while the convoy slowed to a steady twenty five. The system worked well, but then he had been practising quite a lot from his armchair in front of the telly. Brunhilda, fortunately for him, was blissfully unaware of such activities and imagined that this was Silas' first time. 'Impressive', she said grudgingly placing the warm 'Weelief' unit on the floor behind his seat. Silas didn't hear her, he was too busy trying to drive around a tight left-hander with knee against the wheel and to do up his zip without damaging something precious in the process - to him it was, anyway. It would be a fair assumption that at least a hundred people behind him would have bought expensive tickets to see it torn off by a galloping horse.

'Here's our turning Silas, next on the left, only 5 miles to Dawdler's Paradise caravan park now', she beamed. Nearby undergrowth, recently promoted to overgrowth, nearly hid the little sign that said, 'B 666 Stragglers Combe'. Silas was almost sorry to leave the main road, he'd enjoyed the little jaunt, and he'd been counting the cat's eyes and calculating how many to the mile and comparing it with other journeys he'd made. It was a sort of hobby of his, that and mentally calculating fuel consumption.

The liberated traffic sped on past with hell-bent acceleration and intention yet with enough control to glare down the leafy lane with avowed hatred at the back end of the receding Viking Marauder III and make a mental note of the registration ASB01BS as they passed by the B 666 junction and the partially hidden sign that said 'Unsuitable for HGVs or vehicles with trailers'.

On the main road south, the population of the next village had enjoyed a somewhat quieter day than usual and could not believe their eyes when this massive convoy drove in like refugees fleeing from a disaster, many seeking toilets (just locked 5 minutes before) and food and drink from the local shop (closed for at least ten).

In the upstairs back room, unaware and beyond sight of his locked shop door, the local grocer was just sitting down to a frugal tea and confessing to his wife, 'a bad day today dear, only sold a tin of beans and a pasty to old Mrs whatsername from the corner, otherwise no passing trade at all. . . who'd have thought it on a fine day like this'. His wife turned on the 6 o'clock news to see if there had been an accident or road works.

Outside, a few drowsy hypoglycaemic motorists struggled to control their cars, families and eyelids.

Meanwhile, with his caravan touching the hedges both sides of the road; Silas was feeling a lot more comfortable and asked Brunhilda for a sandwich. He felt a lot less comfortable when Brunhilda asked sarcastically, 'and have we washed our hands then?'

'Still', she thought, 'it'll save throwing it away later', and moving the dog ash urns from near her feet where they'd once sat when alive she found the pink Tupperware box, ripped off the lid and pulled out a sandwich with the same hand as had been all round the Weelief bottle earlier. 'There you are then, be it on your head if you die on holiday of some awful disease. . . here's the last chicken sandwich. . . it's a bit warm. . . been in the Sun. . . watch you don't drop bits all over the car, I'm not cleaning it on holiday you know.' As it thwacked heavily into his open left hand the energy rippled through the fat in his body all the way to his gripping right hand and via the steering wheel it finally manifested as a frightening slewing of the caravan which for some 20 yards began to collect clumps of West Country flora and fauna from both roadside banks. 'Eyes on road. . . eyes on road, not your sandwich,' she snapped, thinking, 'dimwit!'

'Soon be there dear,' he mumbled, much to her disgust through a mixture of warm dried chicken, wholemeal seeded bread and saliva. 'And I negotiated a good discount from the owner, Mrs MacGreedy'.

'Well you'd better not have negotiated us into a place next to the bins and toilets again', Brunhilda warned as she picked up her book to read again, as, at 10 to15 miles an hour, it could be some while, especially as the milk tanker they had met in front was having to reverse. Silas didn't say any more about discounts. He realised he was in a bit of trouble now. Mind you, not as much as the tanker driver who was trying to find a farm entrance refuge in his mirrors - proper mirrors too!

Brunhilda thumbed the pages of the book for her place. . . aha! There it was, a page on Rhubarb and vodka crumble recipes. It was a book written by Dennis Thatcher on the use of alcohol in every day recipes. . . absolutely fascinating what could be achieved. . . how to ferment jams for optimum strength. . . Guinness pies, with options to add meat to taste. Port and Sambuca roulade. . . Newcastle brown, cheese and herb pancakes, mmm. . . that Dennis knew how to cook. Dennis and his wife Margaret were their favourite people, in fact swinging about on the caravan wall was a photo of them both and not only that, the Karavanas had named their late miniature Boxer dogs after them. They'd both died reasonably close to old age but somewhat suddenly. . . Silas put it down to them being fed one of Dennis' recipe dinners by accident . . . but he wasn't going to tell Brunhilda that. . . she thought that after they staggered about in the garden and slumped down quietly that they had just been tired then later died peacefully of old age in their sleep. Silas liked it that way as it was his Schnapps and chocolate fudge cake with Ouzo custard they'd eaten. It wasn't his fault; he'd just popped it down by the patio chair while he used the Weelief unit.

At last Dawdler's Paradise was in sight and that nice Mrs MacGreedy was waiting for them at the gate with arms akimbo. As she waved them through the leaning and bramble covered gateway, she shouted through the window, 'You must be Mr Karavana,' she said, ignoring Brunhilda completely, 'you're first on the right, next to the toilet block as you arranged. Electric goes off at nine thirty and back on for eight in the morning. Anything else, see me at the house tomorrow, goodnight, sleep well.'

There was a bird silencing and brooding pre war atmosphere as Silas reversed the caravan in to the allotted place just a few yards from the toilet block and waste bins, in the process nearly knocking some chap over that was emptying his chemical toilet into a nearby open sump. Silas made a mental note not to walk round that side of the caravan in the dark. He was pleased with his parking as he'd done it all on his own without Brunhilda's help or her blessing for that matter.

For the next few days the proximity of the block was to be a blessing in disguise for Silas as the chicken sandwich seemed to carry out Brunhilda's desire for retribution to be visited on the house of Silas, well on his body at least. After a few days of hanging around the caravan … just in case …. Silas had began to browse the 'for sale' section of *Non Stop Caravanning For Middle Englanders*, 'Mmm', he read and thought quietly to himself, 'Caravans for sale, my, I'm pleased with the knock down price I got, even if the cupboard units look like they don't belong in this size van. Mind you, look at some of these foreign ones, still a couple of thousand more. . . ah, the Australian Bonza Croc Mk II and the South African Ridgeback Dominator weren't bad value, nor was the vintage Mk1 Buzzard Scavenger. . . a real beauty in its day'. Silas quickly became fascinated by the extensive section on second-hand toilets and accessories. 'Mmm. . . quality second-hand rear seat commode conversion, fits most Fords'. He was beginning to wonder if they could deliver it to Dawdler's in time for the trip back. As it happened he was better, if not thinner after a week.

They could certainly have picked a better day than the Saturday to scatter the ashes of Denny and Maggie on the beach. It wasn't how they imagined it would be. They'd thought a quiet dignified little private ceremony and then sprinkle the ashes along the shore line. However the wind had got up and a big gust had distributed the remains of their beloved pets across a crowded beach. As the Karavanas made a swift exit, many a small child was asking what the little black bits on their sandwiches were, and young ladies rushed into the sea to wash off dead dog residue that was mottling their sun tan lotion, several people sneezed, including an elderly gent with a big nose all over the bare backs of some teenage lager drinkers. Luckily for them. And dare I say it, the Karavaners too. . . no one knew. . . until now.

How had the Karavana's early victims faired? Not so well I'm afraid, some had gone home early, others stuck it out hardly speaking to each other after the frenzied and uncontrolled breakout of abuse caused by such a frustrating journey. 'Never mind dear, we'll pack up early morning and set off home tomorrow, we'll soon be home and the kids will have their friends, your mum can go home, you can put your feet up and I'll take the dog to the pub. . . it will be fine, you'll see, back to normality'. So after their two week holiday in the sunny south west the family loaded everything into the car, including sheep tics collected by the dog and some sea shells and a couple of dead crabs collected by the children. The parents weren't aware of these extra passengers, not yet anyway, and they set off home ready to enjoy their journey.

Unfortunately at this juncture Mrs Macgreedy was pushing tax-free £5 pound notes into her tartan apron pocket as she was waving goodbye to her guests; Silas cut the corner a bit sharply and bramble scratched the van as he pulled out of Dawdler's gateway, now they, with fresh sandwiches and the comforting presence of an empty Weelief bottle, were on their way home to Hampshire. And only 5 miles to the main road. Not far at all.

'Now look at what you've done to my nice caravan, you were in too much of a rush, showing off to that woman. You needn't think that you're going to drive like a maniac all the way home - you're going to take it steady and I'm going to read my book', informed Brunhilda Adolfina Karavana.

Perhaps you know them? Perhaps you've been behind them. . . perhaps you are them !

Peace lies not in the world,
but in the man who walks the path.

The New Trousers.

It was about time that he smartened himself up. . . So every-one kept telling him. After about 20 to 30 years of dogged, even dog-eared, dog's breakfast resistance, he finally suc-cumbed to the pressure.

He even called at a quality shop for the purchase. It was so difficult to choose for himself as in previous years his wife had taken over from his mother as the sole guide over his wardrobe acquisitions; it was a responsibility to which he had not himself readily taken. It was such a painful struggle emotionally to be in the shop and to know that he couldn't make his mind up about what would look right. Eventually he chose a pair of lightish, darkish, greeny, browny coloured trousers that actually fitted - well, more or less. Now he couldn't even describe the colour to you if he was wearing them - perhaps that was one of his troubles.

The shop assistant folded them neatly and carefully - the last time they were ever to receive such treatment, though to be fair he did use a coat hanger to store them in his cupboard. There they stayed for months while he continued the wear-ing of his various tramp outfits day after day.

Then one day he had an invite to meet a lady for dinner at a pub. He wanted to make a good impression and selected the 'new trousers' as lower body covering and a pair of shoes the wrong colour - but better than his only other option, trainers or wellies.

Upper half coverings slowly stacked up in a growing rejected crumpled heap on the sofa as he searched in vain for something non tramp like - difficult when that is all he had. He had an assortment of tops for gardening, walking, wood collecting and window cleaning ... but nothing much there for going out to dinner. Eventually he settled on something that almost crossed the line in to smart. He posed in front of the mirror. . . 'Mmm, what truly smart trousers', he thought, 'not too bad. . . you look half human. . . an improvement. . . yes. . . that'll do nicely.'

One more admiring glance at the new trousers, so different from the dark stuff he usually wore that didn't need washing for ages, and he turned for the door and the prospect of an exciting rendezvous. Then, one more admiring look of approval, and the door closed behind him.

He met the young lady in question with hope heaped upon hope that his new trousers would impress, even if he didn't. Dinner was eaten, and went well; he carefully avoided anything that might have slopped on to his new trousers. It was, no to spaghetti, no to spare ribs, no to the soup and no to anything with gravy.

It paid off and at the end of the meal it had all gone where intended. . . into his mouth and not down his lovely new trousers. After a while of drinking and pleasantries he felt the need to relieve his bladder of impending pressures. So excusing himself he left the table, being careful not to bump it or skew the tablecloth or to knock a fork to the floor and then, with legs and new trousers in relative harmony, walked an elegant manly-poised walk in the direction of the loo. What efforts we go to, to impress - or rather, perhaps, not embarrass ourselves.

The 'gents' was a fairly modern, posh affair with state of the art taps and driers. Having done what he'd set out to do, he approached the sink to study the tap, which strangely seemed devoid of a handle. 'How odd', he thought, and explored it with his hands. Well, he might have just as well explored it with his groin, for the tap was automated to come on when it detected movement, and a powerful stream of water gushed across the trendy curved and shallow sink bowl. He stepped back quickly, but not quick enough, it was all too late. There in the mirror, clearly shown as a dark patch on the groin of his new light trousers was all the evidence of an 'accident'.

'Oh, God, no', his self screamed to himself, look at that. . . Oh God, no!'; He quickly moved to the hand drier, and forgetting his hands too were wet placed them on his legs and made more wet patches for the world to see.

By now he had been in the loo for several minutes, and his guest must be thinking that he'd climbed out of the window to avoid the bill, or had some sort of undesirable medical problem.

He waved his hands under the drier, waiting for the switch to cut in - but it didn't. Then all of a sudden it did. . . then it cut out again. 'Temperamental B*******', he thought, as mindless panic now racked his entire body and inexorably extinguished any coherent or logical thought. Even when he managed to keep the fan running for a short while, it was obvious that it would require several hours of it to dry the trousers, and he was already on tip toe in an attempt to close the gap 'twixt heater and groin.

It was hopeless; he would have to return through the bar exposed to the world as having wet himself. Now, if he could hold a coat or similar in front of him that would hide the problem, but he had none. He could walk out with both his hands pressed against his groin area, but this would only draw even more attention to his plight and look decidedly more peculiar. 'Oh to hell with it', he thought, 'I bet they've all done this at some time or other, they won't even notice. . . it's all in my mind. . . it will be fine. . . I'll just pretend that nothing has happened.'

As soon as he entered the bar two young girls sitting with their parents sniggered together.

'They're just sharing a joke,' he told himself. In another family a mother put her hands across her child's eyes and whispered in their ear.

'Just playing a childhood game,' he assured his increasingly self-conscious self.

He ignored the old lady nudging her old knitting pals who gestured with a glance in his direction. 'Could be she's spotted an old friend', his mind mumbled to himself. From everywhere he seemed to attract stares, as though he was some superstar celebrity, but no eyes met his - not once. The bar was now eerily quiet, even the music seemed to have stopped to watch.

At least his friend wasn't making a fuss; she didn't even appear to notice as she was intently fumbling in her handbag for a phone. 'Funny', he thought,' I didn't hear it ring.'

'Must dash. . . urgent call', she said standing and grabbing her things in one move. It seemed to him that she was staring intently at the floor, as if looking for something important.

'How odd,' he thought, 'How odd'.

'Must dash, something I have to do. . . bye bye. . . can't stop. I'm going on holiday for a while. . . forgot about it. Bye.'

And she was gone.

He paid the bill. The barman stared openly at his wet patch, 'Hope everything was all right for you sir, please call again,' he said with a slight smirk and a distinct lack of sincerity.

Back home at last and there in the hallway mirror the wet patch stared back mockingly.

'Well it's back in the cupboard for you maties', he announced, and that's where they stayed. . . until. . .

'Say, what are you doing tomorrow night?'

They who only walk on sunny days
never complete their journey

Vietnamese proverb.

Still stuck in the cupboard.

This is a tale of two ageing leather walking boots that share a bond of common past but who have divergent political views.

'Gor blimey, it ain't arf dark and boring in 'ere - and it flippin stinks to boot - if you'll pardon the pun squire,' complained Lefty.

'My, how you commoners complain. It's quite fine over on this side, you probably still have bits of cow dung stuck in your soul', Righty laughed haughtily, with an upper class public school accent. He knew full well what he'd meant with his play on words, and was even as sure that his thick commy colleague didn't.

Mind you, if you knew what they'd been through together you'd not sit in judgement on his humour nor intent.

'Oh, arf, arf, arf, very funny Righty; but seriously, why ain't that bloke thing been to take us out walking. We ain't seen the creature for ages now', retorted Lefty.

Righty always seemed to have the inside information, Lefty reckoned he was a secret Mason of sorts, I mean, why did Righty sport that little decorative stud depicting St Crispin? Stuff like that was all cobblers, and come the revolution, justice would be served, Lefty had visions of the self privileged few spending the rest of their days on building sites doing hard labour. This dream was one of the things that helped him through those long dark days in the cupboard without going stark raving bonkers.

Righty spoke his wisdom, 'Well, comrade Lefty, I think, despite our unstinting and valiant service, we have been discarded on grounds of our age. Because of various and numerous saggings, wrinkles, and bits gone bald; or even missing altogether. I'm afraid we've been discriminated against in favour of a new pair of foreign boots; Chinese I think; state of the art apparel, composite space age soles, breathable waterproof fabric, quintessentially pleasing blue/grey hued suede; soft padding around the ankles. . .'

'I've seen 'em, I've seen 'em', interrupted Lefty, 'What a tarty pair, all swank and no substance; never had their insoles dirtied once with pig slurry, I'll bet.'

'Be that as it may Old Boy', Righty predicted, 'if he's ever planning to walk through pig slurry again you can be sure that we will be re-employed instantly.'

'That bloke thing needs a good lesson in manners then Righty', fumed an incandescently indignant Lefty, who'd been almost completely wound up by Righty's intentional 'bullet making'. 'Pig slurry eh, that's all we're good for eh, well I'll show him. He's going to find his left foot suddenly let him down with a big slip - then he can bathe in pig slurry if he likes the stuff that much.'

There was a long, tangibly charged silence, long even for the cupboard. Righty smirked with success and revelled in the agitation he'd caused his companion. Lefty made contingency plans for falls, slips and trips, in between grunts of rage and periods of silent communist sulking.

The door opened and a thick socked foot came in; the old boots were elated; it was coming their way. Righty was excited, who knows, it may be a grouse shoot up on the moor or a walk on some landed gentry's private estate, or a meal in front of a pub inglenook, oh, how lovely it would be. Lefty was excited too; he had his own dreams, of a different sort to fulfil. . . that mainly involved slurry - any slurry would do.

The socked foot came closer, and then firmly shoved the dreaming pair deeper into the cupboard. Their place was to be taken by a neat little mat, and guess what else. . . Yes, that 'tarty, hoighty toity, la de da pair of suede boots. The now despised bloke thing straightened the suede boots neatly and affectionately brushed a speck of dust off of one toe cap. Then, with a gentle pat and a caress the new boots were gently praised and promised, 'See you soon, my little lovelies'. The door closed, and as the darkness came an even greater darkness fell, somewhere, deeper in the cupboard.

'Bonjour, mes petits amis,' said the new suede boots, twins by all accounts, to the grumpy old brown leather ones in the smelly corner of the cupboard.

'Sorry mate, we don't speaky the Chinese - we're British', retorted Lefty.

Righty smirked again as he saw yet another proletariat cock-up in the making, and said nothing.

'OK, je speaky the eenglish fors yoo, vee are ze Pied sisters from France; vee are appy to be ere. Ow you eenglish say, 'pip pip old boy, tally ho, yoiks yoiks tally ho.'

'Oh Gawd', thought Lefty, 'me jobs been nicked by a foreigner who's resting on that lovely mat that should belong to the people; it's the people's mat, made by the people, for the people - not for some stuck up right wing foreign toff.'

In fact the suede boots were born in China but because they were boxed in France they were issued with a European passport and came over to the UK in the back of a lorry ... quite legally as it happens.

'Huh', muttered Lefty, 'what I'd like to do to that pair; I'd love to get over there and wipe a good dollop of old British cow dung on them'.

'I say, I say, old boy, live and let live; I've taken something of a fancy to the left suede twin', said Righty, adding, loud enough for the whole cupboard to hear, 'she's quite beautiful.'

Lefty fumed, once again successfully fully wound up by his upper class work mate.

Righty's charm had worked its magic and the left suede twin was mesmerised by the admiration and responded with a sultry and alluring accent, 'pardonez moi cher ami. . . ah, forgeev me, exkyoos me dear frend, I kan not elp but admire yor aksent, and kan see yoo are an experienced adventurer of some distinction. Ow you say, 'best foot forward eh?''

'Why you charming young thing you, how kind you are', smarmed Righty, in his best public school accent, 'yes, always best foot forward. . . unless of course it is into pig slurry, and then it is, 'by the left, quick march''. Righty laughed, a private laugh, under his breath.

'Ah, mon dieu, vot iz zees pig slurry?'

'You'll find out soon enough with a bit of luck', thought the scheming Lefty.

Once again silence reigned in the cupboard, now perfumed by exotic Franco Chinese suede and good old British cow dung. Lefty remembered in silence all the sacrifices he'd made for the bloke thing that had used, abused and discarded him. He remembered with pride conquering Snowdon in the mist and Rannoch Moor in the rain; Ben Nevis in cloud and deep snow; he recalled how oft times he had placed himself heroically between danger and the bloke things five headed socked foot, everything from barbed wire, prickly gorse, sharp stones, from soakings in everything from sea water to spring water - and then, of course, there was the pig slurry. Ah, how he remembered the days of his youth, strong and supple, keeping out the icy cold of a frosted Skidaw from that ungrateful bloke thing's foot, sure footed on the treacherous icy slopes, ah, those were the days all right. Once he remembered that he'd been cleaned up and polished for something they called ' the rambler's dinner'. Lefty wasn't sure if it was just his imagination, but he had a feeling that the bloke thing had actually spat on him then rubbed it in with a cloth. Lefty allowed himself a little chuckle as he thought, 'that wasn't half as bad as the time the bloke thing went into the woods to relieve his bladder, but a gust of wind liberally sprinkled most of the contents on to a shocked and incensed upper class Righty.' Lefty remembered with utter glee how he had watched the urine soaked Righty splutter with powerless indignation. Lefty chuckled again, he reminded himself to bring the incident once more to the attention of the cupboard. 'Humph', he thought, 'bet that tarty little suede thing wouldn't admire Righty so much if she knew he'd had a bath in bloke thing urine, arf arf.'

It was Righty who broke the silence first, 'well you little sweeties are you looking forward to your first exploration of the English countryside?' Lefty almost threw up.

'Mon Dieu, vee do not want to get ze vet, vee are, ow vee zay, laisez faire about zis,' explained Tarty. 'If you ask me,' Lefty interjected, even if he didn't know what that means, 'you and that bloke thing will probably need the vet the way you're carrying on. . . and who cares about your fair laces. . . we've got proper leather ones matey.'

Righty despaired: how was he ever going to have his way with that little suede beauty with that left wing moron putting his foot in everything he could. . . yes, including pig slurry and cow dung, it seemed to be a trademark of the cupboard's lower classes.

The right twin spoke for the first time, 'look ere, vee do not like your stinking cupboard, vee are too good for zis place and soon our new pretty young French feet will join us and take us avay from you two miserable bloke thing servant boots. Why anyvun should vont to veezit zis place je ne comprend. . . vot viz ze rain, smelly old cheddar, your little misshapen apples and Yorkshire pudding, every sing is orreeble. Our motto is liberty, egalitie and fraternity. . . But not with the likes of you two.'

As the entire cupboard contents contemplated the wisdom or not of the last conversations their cogitations were to be interrupted by a bright light and expensive French perfume pervading the once ominous darkness. She had arrived, dressed in soft casual pastel coloured clothes she reached out for the 'tarty pair' with squeals of delight and wild laughter interspersed with snorting noises of mid laugh sharp intakes of breath. She, the dainty Angelique, clutched the suede boots tenaciously and possessively to her bosom.

Lefty made a mental note that they were some of the best pig noise impressions he'd ever heard, he looked forward to whatever else the new visitor could do to entertain him.

The bloke thing's hand reached in to the back of the cupboard; The old leather boots felt they were flying like eagles as they were 'flown' to the back door mat; they were not abandoned after all. . . well, not yet anyway.

All four boots were warmed by the car heater as they were being driven off for some wonderful adventure; Righty did not stop talking all the journey, bragging about this Lord's Manor, and that Earl's estate, about grouse and deer, and otter hunts and salmon fishing on private rivers etc and all the things he loved. . . and all the things to which Lefty was vehemently opposed. . . but no chance to speak, just to see . . . and remember. The suede twins merely ignored him as they luxuriated around those pretty socked and wriggling French feet .. oh, how they enjoyed the company, which they sincerely hoped would lead to repatriation. . . and the sooner the better as the right suede boot considered that the incessant old public school ravings of that knackered old English boot could so easily result in her premature deafness.

They had arrived. With the car parked on the crushed granite cliff top view point and the wild Atlantic leaping about as though pleased to see them, they quickly left the exposed cliff for the shelter of some nearby trees; they too shied easterly away from the sea as if to avoid its kiss.

'Right, you two new girls, now you'll get a true taste of adventure; you just stick with us and you'll be sure to have a tale or two to share in the next cupboard you visit', beamed Righty.

Despite the wind it was dry and fairly warm. . . not as warm as the south of France of course, but warm enough; the soft earth path meandered between ancient Beeches and younger Hollies and Silver Birches; they dropped down from the heights into a deeper wooded valley full of the scent of Foxgloves and early Gorse and there, by a little stream running home to the sea, they all sat together on a dry log and the sandwiches were rescued from the rucksack. 'Not that they will appreciate the word rescued,' thought Lefty. The French girl chose to sit on the bloke thing's left as it gave her the best seat and a little shelter from the breeze. This did not please Righty at all, he'd been looking forward to the touch of suede, and now he was furthest away. Lefty smirked smugly, he didn't care where he sat; he had a revolution to plan.

The sensibility and decorum of the occasion dissipated abruptly with the arrival of some strange odour. 'Strewth, blimey O'Reilly, what in Gawd's name is that stink, it's worse than pig slurry', remonstrated Lefty. 'Oh, really Lefty, you do complain so much', said Righty, who had looked up earlier and observed the garlic salami being unwrapped from its special 'nerve gas proof' packaging, 'it's only garlic, it's what the French girl eats.' 'Oh, well,' said Lefty, 'a bit of pig slurry won't bother her then, cos there's some on this path later on, at Waterloo Farm, we've been up here before.'

After a while they were up and off, off up the valley to Waterloo Farm track, which led to the village near the car park. The track was wide and dry with a strip of grass and other plants growing all along its middle. After twenty minutes of pride and pomp by Righty, silent scheming by Lefty, and complete indifference from the French contingent, they approached the farmyard itself; the public right of way ran uncompromising and unfettered, according to the ordnance survey map anyway, straight through the farm. It has to be said that the map did not show the gate, the wire and lake of slurry which separated the two sides of the road. . . the way in, and the way out!

The boots listened to the heated Anglo French discussion high above them. It was a parting of the ways, her new suede boots would never set foot on or in the dastardly English pig slurry. Angelique turned and the tarty pair of suede boots and her skipped jauntily away from the gate and back towards the sea. 'Oh, no!' exclaimed Righty, not only having lost the love of his life but about to be plunged once more in his life into pig slurry, 'that dozy creature has gone too far, he's let his mouth put his body, and us, in a place it doesn't want to be, and now can't wimp out of it. Oh well, I suppose we were born to serve.'

Lefty said nothing. Up and over went the bloke thing, boots swing over the gate and dropped down into ankle deep slurry. 'Mmm,' thought Lefty, 'this is cow slurry, not pig, still it will do'.

There was a scream of surprise and despair from behind her and Angelique stopped and turned to see what it was, and there, just beyond the gate, floundered the bloke thing in slurry.

It was only the twins who could hear the shout of 'traitor' from Righty and the maniacal laughter of Lefty as he shouted, 'up the workers!'

The pretty suede boots shuddered in horror and wondered if they would ever meet those mad English boots again.

Perhaps they will.

Freundelschaft Mountain

An Englishman on a walk, with his imagination
for company, somewhere in the mountains
where they speak German.

It was some two hours earlier that he had climbed steadily
out of the frosted, fog-filled valley, and now he sat in the
warm winter sunshine on an only summer used roadway
surrounded by herds of giant conifer trees. He delved into
his red rucksack and pulled out a paper bag, fresh from the
village bakery that morning, and delving into the paper bag
pulled out a tough clear plastic bag sealed with a glued plastic strip at one end. He very much wished to delve further,
into the plastic bag to retrieve the sandwich, but this bag
wasn't going to give in as easily as the first two. Just like big
Billy goat gruff, this was the third and the tough one. He
picked at the sealing strip with his nails, no good: he looked
around for something sharp, there wasn't; he pulled, with all
his might, to separate the bag at the seal, he couldn't.

Despair; was he to be found dead on the mountain some
days later? His imagination took hold.

'Mmm', said the Doctor, 'Looks like he simply died of
starvation'.

'Ze krazy fool', said the big bearded guy from mountain
rescue, 'ze idiot should have eaten ze sandvitch he has got in
his hands.' Under his breath he mumbled something about

the mountains being no place for namby pamby, townie day trippers, especially foreigners.

However, this was not to be, eventually the bag split near the seal and from then on, no matter what he did, he couldn't stop the bag splitting. He'd thought of only eating half the sandwich but in trying to extricate the half he wanted the once invincible plastic bag surrendered at every turn. He ate the whole sandwich and studied the plastic bag with a forensic scrutiny for a while before thoughtfully placing it in the rucksack.

The aforementioned culinary delight, which in itself had contained a few surprises too, was purchased in a shop where no English was spoken. I t was a bit of a lottery which one of three sandwiches on display were to be his. He'd understood that there was meat in them - but what meat? Sticking his fingers to his head like cow's horns, he 'moo'd', much to the consternation of the gathering group, now swelled by the shopkeeper calling a couple of assistants - to assist - but they couldn't! He mooved on, and made donkey noises; the female shopkeeper responded quickly with a more feminine 'eeh awh', and pointed to the central round bun with a hint of salami sticking out the side. 'I'll have the other one then', he said hurriedly pointing to the one without donkey, 'whatever it is, I'll have that one please.' They all nodded in approval in their own language, and the said sarnie was removed to the mountain forest via the red rucksack. It was tasty, he had to admit, though he was never sure, even under close scrutiny, what meat it was, but it went well with the sliced pickled gherkin and pieces of boiled egg he'd found hiding half way through. Yet one more surprise on the mountain

Suitably replenished he followed the instructions of a woodcutter he had chanced upon earlier on the climb; they'd been given in staccato bursts of broken, almost obliterated, English with a strong Teutonic accent. 'Go zis vay, (points left), zen zis vay up, (points right and makes gesture of uneven ground, which he discovered later meant steps up);

Ven yoo kum to ze street, (rarely used forest tarmac road), go zis vay, (points left) 300 metres (paused long while as he fitted his memory to the instructions) zen up into ze forest. Zen anuzzer street, (which he never found) zis vay to ze big vooden hauze, (which he did find) zen up ze forest - und zen yoo vill be at ze top. (Pausing thoughtfully) About vun hour, vun hour kvorter.'

Some two and a half hours later he was still stumbling through worsening forest conditions on steep ground.

His imagination took hold again - he imagined that the woodcutter had covertly smiled somewhat knowingly as they had parted company, one to stay with his fire and log pile and one to wander aimlessly in a wooded purgatory. Had the woodcutter been fondling his father's iron cross in his pocket as he 'guided' the English visitor?

Ze Teutonic Gazette reports, '*Englander lost for days in remote mountain forest. Local hero and woodcutter, Adolf, Kaiser Von Richthoven said, 'I met zis foolish Englander on ze mountain. I begged him to return to ze safety of ze valley. I could do no more, I vood haf guided him but I had to look after my sick grandmutter und deliver zum eggs to ze orphanage. Mine farzer vos right, zeze Englanders vill never listen.'*

However, it worked out all right, the instructions were good, though distances were confusing as path after path appeared, and then, when he chose one to follow, that too would fork and give another choice. As for timings, the woodcutter's family must have had a long line of national decathlon athletes in their genes.

It was following one of the path choices that he found himself on a steep bank that looked directly down on to the path on which he should have been; in fact it was a track he had been on earlier but in his inimitable wisdom had abandoned! As he, unlike any proper mountain walker, edged his way down the banking on his backside, feet scrabbling for some tiny grip and gloved hands at the ready to hang on to any convenient thistle or blade of grass, a small dog appeared on the track and began to laugh. . . I mean, bark at him. 'Hallooo old doggy', he said, and then he saw them, a whole group of well equipped, fit mountain walkers, (probably in light training for the Eiger north face). They must have marvelled at his novel descent skills, probably joking amongst each other, 'I vunder if he vill teach me his vunderbars technik', 'Nein, vee must not disturb him, he iz probably a master mountain guide collecting ze infermazion for his latest book'. They all smiled at him as they came by. . . or were they laughing? He took no chances and, in order to create distance between them he held back, pretending to be looking at everything . . . and anything. . . with great interest, the view, the sky, the plants. . . even his boots.

Well above the mist now and in a bright sunshine that lit the grey flat swathe of mist that levelled out the valley below, he contemplated his onward journey.

As he trekked doggedly nearer his goal it would be nice to say his boots bit into crisp higher altitude snow, but we cannot, as the snow was so ice hardened that each step on the forty five degree slope was a slippery test of resolve; and it was easier going up! Coming down the iced snowy mountain was likely to be much quicker - even if unintentionally!

He found the 'pub' at the summit, (one of the better Teutonic ventures), and had a soup made of stuff he didn't recognise, served by a waitress he couldn't understand. One of the frequent delights for the traveller of foreign lands - 'here comes ze lone tourist, kvick get zer old Yak genitals from zer freezer, he vont know vot he orders, heh heh.'

Many of the snowy bits on the way down caused, what is known in mountain trade circles, as the 'whoops' feeling, almost instantly followed by ancient Anglo Saxon words of surprise, and a quick shot of adrenalin. The good thing about walking alone is that you are the only one witnessing your clumsy, pathetic and frightened progress; embarrassment becomes a solitary pleasure!

He survived; back in his friend's apartment, kettle on and biscuits found, he rested on the long comfortable settee. . . as he lay warm, the tea went cold and he drifted into a gently fatigued snooze. . . was it a dream or the news on the TV he could hear: 'Freundelschaft Mountain graced by presence of heroic English walker. . . conquers local summit in bad weather. . . survives on only one sandwich . . . saves humble woodcutter from certain death. . . carries him down mountain before returning to the summit, '. . . zzzz . . .'.

'It is not because things are difficult that we do not dare.
It is because we do not dare that they are difficult.'

Life. . . the way it is. . . or was.

Hotel Illustrious

The dubious pleasure of a night's stay 'somewhere' in England.

It was late in the old Hotel Illustrious, and he downed his 'complementary' Suchard's hot chocolate drink and lay on the bed. It was a double – when he had booked it was only a fiver extra for a big bed so he'd taken it. It also meant there was plenty of space too – except in the shower as he was later to discover.

He'd stayed there before, only in a single, and this new room was no quieter than the first, as again Friday night teenagers raced the streets below, showing the world just how fast they could drive in town; he wondered if Fittipaldi, Schoemaker and Lauda grew up here.

He looked around the room and his eyes examined the emergency fire exit in the corner. 'FIRE EXIT' it said in the middle of the narrow door, and in a small glass panel with an attached chain and little hammer, it proclaimed, to the interested, how it could be opened.

'Good job I read it now,' he thought; 'if the lights had failed, then the instructions would be just as much in the dark as I would be.' The secured door led to another guest's room, later he would be putting his ear to it to locate 'the voice'.

In the opposite corner was a similar looking door but now obviously viewed from the other side. Though he'd booked in alone, if the alarm was to sound (presuming they had one that functioned) that night he could well have visitors – even if they were just passing through. In 1845, the hotel brochure proudly proclaimed, the place had partially burned down – he suspected that a fire today might well improve considerably on the word 'partial'. He could see the light from the hallway shining where the smoke would come above and below his closed door. The exit door from the neighbours was blocked by a big easy chair. Throughout the Hotel, and the night too, as it happened, all fire doors were neatly and securely propped open with a heavy object – the fire extinguishers; it was a long bone breaking and probably fatal drop to the street three floors below.

Earlier he had put the huge ' bet you won't forget me' hotel key fob in his pocket and walked to a small village pub with his cousin who lived in the town.

'What's your favourite then?' he asked the landlord as he eyed the chalkboard menu. He thought to himself, 'the landlord should have a good idea as it's his wife out the back cooking'. It was a toss up between the hot chicken curry with rice and the moussaka. 'The curry is hot', the landlord warned, 'but very nice'. His cousin ordered 'moussaka' and he, against his instinct, ordered the curry. They were on their second pint by the time the food arrived and it was immediately evident which was best value – that damned moussaka was!

Blast, he thought, 'I knew I should have had that'.

How right he was, and how right the landlord too is on his judgement on the wife's curry being 'hot'.

'Thank the Lord for cold Guinness', he thought, as he tried to cool his tongue from the effects of the first forkful. They had their third pint along with the 'puds', or sweets as the posh seem to call them, then it was a carefree saunter back into town along the peaceful village lane.

'One more for the road' was had in the pub next door to his hotel and they were entertained by the activities of a loud group of party girls courting inebriation ready for the club scene later.

Back in the hotel, on passing the lounge, he exchanged some unintelligible conversation with the owners, his partial deafness in both ears not helping over-much with the strong Italian influence that inhabited the owner's English.

Up in his room, (which he was pleased he'd managed to find again, what with the combination of little stairways and changes of direction), he put the kettle on. While the seem ingly one watt kettle slowly warmed itself and its contents he squeezed himself into the 'smallest room' for a wash. Yes 'squeezed' is the right word.

To close the door he had to wedge himself between sink and loo; with door closed the tiny shower cubicle was revealed along with a space to stand at the sink. The place seemed to have only one advantage, if you were really ill you could sit on the loo and be sick in the sink at the same time – 'a dubious advantage for a hotel room', he thought.

He must have eventually fallen asleep – in the bed, not the smallest room – as he was awoken by a man's voice; it was 12.33 on the hotel's bedside clock. He tried to ignore the voice, that of a man, fairly deep and almost expressionless as though reading out loud a letter, but the letter became a book and the book became a play, so much so he wondered if it was an actor rehearsing his lines. There was neither reply nor any other voice, even if there was it would not be heard above the loud and boring man's extolations; 'the voice' had the apparent skill to continue speaking endlessly without seemingly stopping for breath.

He left the bed and wandered the night darkened room trying to locate the source, so loud that the speaker might have actually been in the room, perhaps sitting in the chair that blocked the escape route. No, the voice was coming from the room beyond the flimsy 'FIRE EXIT'. Having assured himself it was not within his own walls he returned to bed. As he pulled over the heavy duvet his mind went to what seemed another world. . . to the soft comfort of his bed back home and plans for his spiritual advancement.

It was not possible to sleep with the droning fiend next door still going on as fresh as when he first started – and still not breathing either! In desperation he knocked rapidly on the adjoining wall in the hope that at least one knock would arrive in between words; no luck! He tried again and considered if he should get up, dress and try and find the neighbours room in the timber catacombs of hotel Illustrious. He decided against it and gave three good thwacks with his fist against a new piece of wall.

………SILENCE……..

He tried to sleep but had allowed himself to be so aggravated by the need to do such a thing in the first place, plus that now awful 'silence'. Would it be followed by footsteps and creaking boards and a knock on his own door?

In the event he slept fitfully all night, well nearly all night, until awoken by his neighbours at 6.17 on the hotel clock and the sound of bathroom activity. At 7.47 by the little red numbers of the clock he was up and on his way to the little room, where in the dim electric light he glimpsed what seemed a half human but friendly face smiling back at him from the mirror.

He was first in for breakfast and met by that strong accent which enquired if he would like, 'owse'. 'Sauce?' the deaf one asked. 'No, owse!' 'Salt?' 'No, owse, weeth brahn orwa wyta breada'. 'Aha, TOAST, yes please, brown bread, thank you'.

He was as relieved at the outcome as was the perplexed owner.

He sat in a corner seat to watch the world – and who knows catch a glimpse of the body that entombed the voice of the night.

A couple came in, but the owner had put on the radio – so he couldn't work out if this man's voice was the 'one from the night'. The man was talking quietly now in the breakfast room; his partner was likely foreign from the way he spoke to her and her difficulty with the menu.

It was fascinating to watch as the owner, now with fully awake and functioning Italian accent, asked what they wanted for breakfast. After many exchanged strange words and expressive gestures the owner went away with the impression that they wanted two full English breakfasts – sadly he wasn't there to see the result.

Full English breakfasts were true to their word – plenty of it, sausage, bacon, eggs, mushrooms, tomato, beans, the works. He was nearly finished when he felt something dig in along his tongue – 'mmm', he mused, 'that feels like a hair'. The couple were busy with each other and the owner and accent were out of sight, he foolishly thought he'd be able to grip the offending item with thumb and forefinger and check it out, but it seemed anchored in some other part of the mouth's contents and proved elusive and steadfast. The choice was his; he'd have to act soon, just swallow and move on or avail himself of the serviette. He tried to move the contents around to obtain a better location – all to no avail. 'Right, it's got to go', he ordered himself and so saying the serviette became a new and secret safe house for whatever it was.

Last forkful of bacon and sausage off the plate checked ok, he popped it in his mouth and moved on to the toast and marmalade. He thought, in Russian, 'eta safdrec bila ochin fcosna, balshoi spasiba'. (*This breakfast, very tasty that was, many thanks*)

Now washed, changed, packed and the room checked for spare £20 notes he might have mislaid, he said a cheery goodbye at reception to the landlady – with no complaints.

Let's face it he might want to come back one day!

**

One thought alone can stop a thousand.

**

A fairy story, with magic, tragedy and adventure.

It was late, the rain swept road lit by his lone car headlights as he took the old road through hills and trees towards the sea and home. Beautiful, soul touching music filled the air from the car's speakers, and though not easy to discern the words, it mattered not, for the rise and fall of tones in her Scots voice sent the story of the song direct to the soul.

It was the sort of road and the sort of song that spirits your heart and soul to younger years, to a world of hopes and dreams entangled in the memories of life and love's realities. Music that wakes the very life force that fires the spirit to all that is brave and noble, invoking feelings that inspire the ordinary to greatness; feelings that were you to try and describe would melt away , for they themselves know they cannot be shared, for they belong to you, alone.

As he listened, his mind drifted to thoughts of a story he had half wanted to tell.

One part of him said, 'Tell it, tell it, it is a story of magic, love and tragedy, it's worth the telling, tell it!' Another in him spoke also, 'but if you do, it will not be easy, for you will find demons to fight along the way. If you tell it, then everyone may know you and judge you and all the things you would want not from the telling.'

As his journey travelled with the clock, hour by hour, so his inner conversation continued; brilliant ideas and flowing moving words would appear, then a darkness of fear and doubt cover them over. Then, one winter evening shortly after his return home he picked up his pencil and he wrote...

'The Princess and the China Bell'

'Where on Earth do you start old boy?' he asked himself.

Himself replied, 'Just any where will do. Don't worry if you miss something out, if you wait for perfection you'll never do anything. Why not start with your early trips to Russia?'

Some ten years earlier his long held dream of going to Russia came true when his Martial arts teacher, and indeed good friend, was invited to teach there. He had no wife at the time and lived alone, dedicated to his work in the Fire Brigade and absorbed by the Aikido he practiced with like-minded people. This was seemingly all life had to offer at the time.

Russia was good to him, welcoming, and flowing with food and vodka - at least where they were it was. He was to go there several times, normally during autumn or spring when the five month snows still covered the land. One of the high-lights of the visits was the family gathering meal times; he would sit at the table surrounded by fellow students, teach-ers and family of the hosts. The feeling of welcome, of fami-ly, was like coming home, and so different from his empty house back in England.

Much vodka was drunk and many toasts were made. Once you had a full glass, which was almost constantly, you could raise it and say, 'Toast', and all present would stop and listen. It was your chance to speak of great things or little things, to inspire with poetic grace the gathered company to lift their glasses and drink with the joy of fellowship.

Two years into these regular visits to Russia he noticed among the many students a young woman who stood out from the crowd, short, pretty and exceedingly smart and cleanly dressed, long blond hair in a plait under a skewed brown beret. She was a dedicated student of the art and was often used by the teacher to demonstrate throws.

Another year or two go by and the same little woman stood quietly, now with shorter and darker hair, in a corridor at a sports camp in the snowy forests of north west Russia. She smiled her lovely smile and looked up quietly at him while the men spoke, for there it was the domain of men to rule and speak. Although by now she was the force behind organising the events for the visiting teacher it was not her place to enjoy any of the benefits. While the men drank and sang heroic Russian songs in the sauna and tucked into fresh kebabs cooked in the snowy forest over a living fire, she was somewhere else.

Often small gifts would be exchanged between visitors and their hosts, but one such gift in particular was to have a special place in his life. She offered the small wrapped gift and as he opened it he saw it was a pretty little china doll, but more than this, it was a bell. He rang the little china bell and asked, 'When I ring this bell, will you appear?'

Next to his old armchair, bought cheaply in a farm yard sale, in his home in England stood an old bookcase that his late father had acquired for him for a tenner; on the shelves were various mementos of people, places and family, and among them sat the pretty china bell, and sometimes, as he sat in his aloneness, he would pick up that bell and ring it gently, and wish.

More visits and more years passed their way and each time he would see her smiling face again, always helpful always friendly. 'Such a nice girl', he thought.

Then, one year, she came to England, to stay for three months as a live-in student at the Aikido training centre (dojo). He was to see her often now as he trained there as much as he could with his teacher. It had always been his habit to befriend all the visiting students, taking along good food for them and where possible taking them out on sight seeing visits, and it was no different for her. Boating, shops, museums and botanical gardens; and their friendship grew.

She confided in him of her life in Russia, of an alcoholic mother, sister on drugs and the murder of her only cousin in his own flat; of long hours of work with poor pay and no prospects, and little chance of true freedom and happiness. Although she was young and strong she suffered from stresses and health problems and he did his best to help her overcome them. Their friendship grew more and more strong and turned to love, a love that they could not show to the world, and even then complaints were made to the teacher by some who believed this relationship was harmful to the peace of other students.

They hatched a plan whereby each time they might be lucky enough to spend time alone they would say ,'hallo', and each time before they re-entered the training place they would simply say 'goodbye' to each other. They gave no outward signs of their love but had secret signals in the training hall whereby they could reassure each other of continued affection. Though there was much to gain by this relationship there too was much to lose.

The huge gap in their ages was a great source of embarrassment and despair to him, more, he sensed, than to her; the sort of feelings that few on the outside of them would ever understand. On those very rare occasions when they were free of the martial arts centre their talk was always open and honest; there was an implicit trust in each other. Fears grew that it would soon be goodbye, as her visa came closer to expiry; they imagined a fantasy world in the future when, being reborn to a new life, they could meet again and be the same age; he was to live in China in the foothills of some great mountain and would be, of course, an accomplished martial artist, she was to be a pretty Chinese princess and they would meet again and feel the same way, unburdened by the weight of age.

Phone calls from Russia mounted pressure as they insisted, cajoled and begged, for her return, such foreboding calls were never welcome. They comforted each other as the emotional torture worsened.

In all his years in the Fire Brigade he had never carried out that 'heroic, dream rescue', which so many hope will be theirs. Yes, he had always been willing to place his body between the danger and the helpless, but to know for certainty that he had directly saved a life had eluded him despite those long years of dedication. In his mind it was as though he was at the head of a ladder looking into a brightly burning house, into which he could not enter, and in the room she simply stood. In his mind he reached out a strong hand to save her, but he could not reach her, she must reach out too, to be saved. Many a time this dream would come to him and each time the girl would turn her back and quietly and silently disappear into the burning room. Then, one day, she did reach out and he knew at last he had saved a life. Against much opposition and all advice they realised only marriage would keep her from a return to a dangerous world of little hope and unhappy future.

One autumn day they set off together to the mountains of north Wales; her own, native land was vast but flat, snow covered for five months then swamp and forest during the thaw followed by a very short hot summer, so mountains had excitement and magic in them. As they sat on Snowdon's summit he took a ring from his pocket and asked, with hope and with fear if she would marry him. She thought quietly for a few minutes, while he sat and waited, then turned and said that she would. They stayed a short while on the summit then set off on the long trek down. They had not gone so very far when they looked down into a cloud filled valley below to their right. Behind them the Sun shone brightly casting the shadow of the ridge path on the clouds below, and there amidst a circular rainbow stood their shadows, one tall, one short; they waved down and their shadows waved back, then the clouds drifted away and the wonder was gone, like all that fades in life, leaving only memories.

She secretly journeyed back to Russia where she met up with her mother and father in order to say goodbye properly; it was already too late to see her grandmother who had sadly passed away in her absence. She returned to England where they were married quietly with only another retired fire officer and his wife for witnesses. It was a private affair of necessity. They made their home in his old bungalow and were rarely separated. He had the habit of calling her, 'a little sweetie', which she promptly adulterated to, 'swootie'. To their friends they became known as the 'Swooties' much to everyone's amusement. One day, while sitting at the old pine kitchen table as she prepared a huge saucepan of brilliant tasting soup, he asked her what her wishes for life were. She replied, 'a house by the sea, chickens and a dog'. This had been his dream too for many, many years and he knew it was within his reach. Sometimes when it comes to making a dream real it is not so easy, so, no dog, no chickens, but the house near the sea was on. Not long after this they moved to the land of his ancestors in the South West, he practiced his martial arts and to him she was his Princess.

She studied and worked hard. For a couple of years there was much happiness and they did the silly things you do when uninhibited, childlike happy things like dancing round the living room and singing aloud some silly made up songs.

Then she found a dream of her own, a dream that would take her away to fulfil her ambition hundreds of miles away. A melancholy fell over the house and the writing was on the wall, though none of it bitter, only sad. He had saved her life for freedom, now freedom beckoned her away.

As she gathered her belongings into cardboard boxes she eventually came to the little china bell. She held it in her hands and looked up, saying, 'You won't be able to keep this, will you?' She knew it would be a constant reminder of the fairy story that once was, a story of gain and loss. He kept back the tears and said, 'No, you take it'.

So, the little bell has gone, no longer there to ring again in his aloneness to call her back. And though life moves on, the memory still remains.

The story could end there, but while we live we can live to change the ending and some months later he went to China with a martial arts group of travellers and in a Temple in the foothills of Wudang Mountain he knelt and silently, in front of some great statue, told his story of the Princess and the china bell; adding that he had no plans yet to die, in order to meet his princess in a new life.

The young Chinese girl, who was their guide on the mountain, gave him quite a surprise when she said her Chinese name but that most people called her, 'Sweetie'. For some unknown reason, as he waited with the group leader, last to board their train, she gave him an impromptu hug. Perhaps this meeting with 'Sweetie' fulfilled the lovers bargain, only time will tell.

As he put down the pencil he was grateful to the other in him that had written his story for he could not have done so, and he hoped that in the life he had saved lay the power to save many more.

He was tired now and as he closed his eyes to sleep he smiled with gratitude for all those very special happy times he had spent with his little princess and her china bell.

Only those who once walked the path together and who stood their ground together know the truth.

'If you don't keep quiet sometimes, you will never hear the echo.'

'Greengates' - a fire and a life - so what?

About an ordinary man in extraordinary circumstances, his feelings and his actions at a dangerous fire

He was a younger man than now as he stood on the night-time gravel road by the big red engine. It was an isolated place far from the lights of the City, but it had its own light as a fierce fire swept through the workshops and cars of Greengates scrap yard.

The gates themselves were indeed green, big solid gates, higher than most men could ever see over. They were locked fast against intruders, of any description, good or bad. The younger man stood, and was fully conscious of his thoughts that reflected on life and death. At this time in his life neither of them had any importance, neither life nor death mattered at all.

Up and over the gates, strong arms first pulling and then pushing his body over to the other side; Heavy fire boots dropped into the fire lit compound, it was only then he thought, 'guard dogs', but thankfully none appeared. Soon hose and branch were passed over from the men on the outside, and one other joined him, Paul, a good colleague. With a shout for 'water on', they advanced the heavy hose across the compound hitting the fire where experience had taught them did the most damage.

The all devouring fire roared and crackled, bright flames lit up the poisoning black smoke pouring into the winter night sky. Closer still they went, closer still to slay their enemy dead. In amongst the glowing workshop fire, the pressure was building in industrial cylinders; he was well aware of the dangers of such, on occasion bursting like bombs, throwing flame and hot metal in all directions.

Still alone, and closer still they went; then a heavy loud 'crump' and the ground burst instantly into light all around. The younger man crouched lower still, not daring to look up to see what might be coming down. Life or death mattered not, but pain did; he could still feel that, burns were a horror they all respected and avoided at all cost. Would this demon fire fall, like the angel of death, from the heavens and engulf this crouching figure in the yard?

He waited; it was to be life, and life with no pain; after the fright now it was their turn and onwards they pressed, now supported by more colleagues and after many labours and many hours the demon was finally slain dead, though it had taken much with it while it lived.

Still, to him, this younger man than now, life nor death mattered naught, but survival with honour would do him for a while.

Author in 1984 about the time of Greengates Fire. The story was written at the time.

Fagin and the Banker
A tale of social justice.

Amongst the throng of Victorian peasants in a narrow London street, the Toff was a seething frenzy of pompous anger, in fact he was twice angry. He'd had his pockets picked whilst brow-beating a poor and needy shopkeeper over a particular item he envied and of which he alone knew the true value, and now what was about to be his for a pittance, yes, *all his*, was not to be. All because of some despicable thief who had spirited away his wallet. It never occurred to him he may have misplaced it, nor that the poor shopkeeper desperate to feed his family was out of a sale, no matter how poor the price he might have accepted.

The Toff knew a bargain all right and how to squeeze the last drop of blood from a desperate seller. It was his business after all. He wasn't short of a few bob, why, he had plenty more back at his mansion behind the grand iron gates and high stone wall. His estate sported all that money could buy - mostly other people's that is, for he was a Banker, and immensely proud of this achievement.

He'd done so well for a man with no qualifications, he'd made good by using a brutal disregard for justice and the common people. Why? Don't they have the workhouse for those sorts and had he not always been so generous at Christmas time; on Boxing Day he'd always sent the workhouse big heaps of his Christmas day's leftovers for them to sort through.

The Toff was angry. He called for the police, who on arrival would faun and suck up to him like their lives depended on it - and their livelihood probably did!

'We'll do our best M'lud, we'll try and catch the culprit', said one nervously.

'Well let me tell you, you'll do more than that; how is an honest man like myself supposed to walk the street in safety while you sit on your lazy backsides and let criminals own the streets,' he fumed, in a la-di-dah voice that drew a crowd, 'your chief Constable is coming to dine with me on Sunday and you can be sure he'll be hearing all about this sorry episode. What's your name?'

Not so far away down a side street in a garret hovel a small scruffy man endured a somewhat more frugal existence, his name was, Fagin.

Fagin - now there's a man the Police would not think to treat so kindly; not only was he the enemy of the rich but he was relatively powerless himself and could never command rich lawyers to protect him - and incidentally it was most unlikely they would meet the Chief Constable having lunch there!

Just what was Fagin's crime? Apart from living simply and frugally - no mansion for him, no fine clothes; let's see, - well, though he used young children, often orphans, he provided them with a home full of companionship and camaraderie - he provided food for them better than the workhouse ever could, they were relatively safe, they were off the streets and had a roof over their heads. Not only this, but Fagin would invest time in entertaining and educating his young charges, in effect providing an apprenticeship for young people at a time when there was little but the slavery of servitude for those outside. He helped and mentored them to grow strong and be able to fend for themselves; he provided clothing for them from his own little 'co-operative' business.

He was also in his own way the equal of the great socialist reformers - he was engaged in the redistribution of wealth. On a small scale perhaps, but on a larger scale he would have been the envy of many a true socialist Prime Minister.

Fagin's little empire thrived, providing employment, security and housing for the poor ; his own fortune increased but so did his worries, the more he had the more he feared its loss. He kept his savings hidden under a loose floorboard, but fearing its discovery by some common thief decided to invest it in a bank.

'Yes', Fagin thought with glee, that he'd found a solution to his worries, 'That's what I'll do, I'll stick it all in the bank - it'll be safe and snug in there!'

Written at the time of bank collapses
but big bonuses; a prelude to recession

'What we deeply cling to imprisons us.'

The Yuletide Logs

and how to burn what took
you the whole summer to chop.

I must have been in my mid thirties; I was working as a fire-man and living in a little village bounding the edge of a river that ran through the flat fenland countryside of Cambridgeshire. In the village there lived and worked a family that built sheds and almost anything else wooden, they also owned a piece of low lying riverside land at the far end of which stood the remains of a couple of old Elm trees. These ancient Elms had succumbed to the Dutch Elm disease but had the potential to be turned into logs and then money.

It was a simple agreement; the owner would supply a chainsaw and axe, and I would supply the labour and my old gardening trailer; we would then share any proceeds. Mostly I could drive my old car and trailer along a track to be close to the trees but after heavy rain you'd need a tractor or tracked vehicle to journey the quarter mile or so from road to tree.

Such a day it had been just before one Christmas Eve, and the 'guvner' informed me that we had an order for a trailer load from a man in the next village for 'Yuletide logs' to warm his cosy family Christmas. Nothing daunted, always willing to help, I set off with car and trailer, leaving them on hard standing by the field gate near the road, and I carried the chainsaw and fuel along that soaked, puddle filled, slippery mudded track. Look, the word track is too generous, it was simply a poor field edge too awkward to cultivate that had been deeply rutted by the odd tractor. I set to, that cold wet winter's day, and cut large lumps of wood and branches to a size that I could only just about carry on my shoulders. I carried those heavy timbers one by one, back and forth, and back and forth along that 'track', slipping, straining, and giving it all for this man's Christmas logs. Eventually the trailer was full. Mud and all, I set off for the village yard where the owner had his business. Once there I lifted the timbers from the trailer and cut them into fire log size pieces before splitting with the axe to reveal the beautiful dark swirls of knotted Elm. Not easy work this knotted wood as by now all the easy bits had been sold off ... but a family man in the next village is looking forward to this treasured bounty to brighten his family's Christmas Day. Logs lifted yet once more and reloaded, I set off to find the address, after a short search I found the house and approached the door. 'Bing, Bong' the bell went, 'your logs are here', I said, by now it being mid afternoon of the 'Eve'. 'Good, I've been waiting, you can put them in the garage,' the unsmiling man said pointing to the garage door at the top of the drive.

I reversed the trailer closer to the garage and began unloading those precious spiritual Christmas Yuletide logs, the centuries old fruits of mother earth and human toil. 'Thud, thud, clonk, clonk' they went as I hurriedly transferred them from trailer to garage floor - for, I too, had some hopes of a tolerable, if not happy, Christmas Eve.

'Clonk, clonk, clonk' went the logs into plastic bags as the nearly new owner frenziedly tried to keep up with me. For the life of me I could not understand what he was doing, had he asked I would have gladly put them in the bags for him, but no, he was totally engrossed feverishly clonk, clonk, clonking the logs into his big plastic bags. Most odd, he was seemingly devoid of the Christmas cheer that those hard won logs were supposed to have brought him. Isn't that why he wanted them?

Then the penny dropped; there was a small clue in what he said next; 'Not many here for a trailer load is there? I expected more than this.' He'd been counting the logs all along. 'Not sure they're worth fifteen quid'. Was he after a discount? He wasn't going to get one from me I can tell you; I would gladly have laboured a little longer and taken them all back to the yard for a more deserving customer. I think he must have sensed my disappointment at his displeasure that cold, wet Christmas Eve. 'Humph, oh well, it's too inconvenient to get them elsewhere at this late hour, here's your money, but I won't have any more from you' so saying handing over £15 exactly, of which for my efforts half was to be mine. So with nearly a day's seriously hard labour behind me and with my body's life no doubt shortened by about a week, I took his money.

'Thank you' said I, 'and a Merry Christmas'.

As I drove away I thought, 'not much Christmas spirit there old boy, not much at all, not even a smile ... he'd have smiled all right if he'd carried those logs for miles through the mud.' Poor old logs, I wonder how he put them on the fire, did he pick them up with gratitude in his heart for the tree's great sacrifice, was there a silent prayer of reciprocal warmth as he placed them on the burning embers?

It is one Christmas Eve I'll not forget; not so much for the labour, the day or the fetching of the logs but the handing them over to endure abject slavery and an arboreal purgatory to boot.

That day the man from the next village had forever burned more than simply firewood.

'He not busy being born is busy dying'
Bob Dylan

The Yuletide Logs
30 years on

Now in his early sixties, the call for Yuletide logs fell upon him once again.

He'd seen the giant log earlier in the month while walking with a friend along a tidal river's companion footpath. The 'log' was almost a tree, on closer inspection it was old and dry, despite being touched by the occasional spring tide that would flow a few miles upstream. It was probably the river that once carried his tree to its resting place just yards down the stony banked slope of the long disused railway track, and separated from the main river by a hundred yards or so of salt marsh. The 'log' was probably thirty yards long and a good foot across at the thickest end; it had locked itself by thinner but usable branches into the estuary mud and under the shelter of a row of weather stunted track side trees that overhung the marsh.

Wood burner stoves had changed much in thirty years and were increasingly popular due to a steeply rising price in gas and electricity. A fuel shortage in the world seemed imminent. In North Devon a log shortage also seemed imminent according to regular log burning enthusiasts in the pub as they reported sparse finds on their forays into the wilderness. All the easy wood was gone, collected, cut, chopped and no doubt already burned by new owners of log burners, all fearing that the wood was running out, and of course the evidence was all around; previously rich in pickings logging grounds were now only populated by the empty handed log hunters themselves.

The 'log', our log. . . his log, was so far safe, but for how long? It was a good mile away down the track from where his car could be parked. Christmas was coming and coming apace; the log must be saved from marauding Yuletide log snatchers. He must act.

He had lunch in the Royal Hotel, changed into old clothes in the car park, donned woolly hat and gloves, picked up the trusty bow saw and set off steadily westward on the winter frosted track.

It seemed to be further along than he remembered as his eyes scanned the tidal debris hiding under the bank and trees; fortunately the log's position was roughly land marked by a big white house across the river on the opposite bank and it was a relief to find his log still there.

Less nimble. . . if he ever had been nimble. . . and so as not to slip with it in hand he threw the saw through the broken wire fence on to the salt-marsh below, then he carefully worked his body under the rusty but still stout British Rail fencing wires, his feet now with a will of their own sliding down the steep slope; he hung on to the wire with his hands; the whole process, to a casual observer, resembling the activities of an inebriated orang-utan in tramps clothing; at last he obtained an upright posture, feet firmly settling into the salt marsh mud.

There she was, the log, the great log, half hidden under fresh tide delivered flotsam; he used his ageing strength and weight to roll the log for a convenient cut.

Convenient cut? The bow saw struggled to make any effect on the hard wood; even the low angle of cut had the tip of the saw driving into the estuary mud. . . in good company with his boots and knees. He stopped several times to stand, rest and stare up and down the river as if doing so would materialise the chainsaw and trailer needed for this job. Neither appeared and thought alone wasn't going to cut the log so he struggled on slowly and cut twice so as to give him two good pieces and leave enough for three more another day. He dare not cut the remainder for fear of pillagers taking advantage.

No, it was best left in one big awkward lump, he covered the evidence with a little mud and few leaves and orang-utanged his way back up the slope and on to the track.

Now the mile trek with heavy burden back to the car.

About halfway he was stopped by an old lady out for a walk, she enquired of directions as to how she could return to the town by a different route. She was in no rush to ask, or to hear the answer, obviously the chap in front of her could stand there all day holding those logs on his shoulder. He gave her his best advice and continued the step by step struggle homewards. A dog came by, with a keen look at his logs. He'd noticed before that dogs, often out that way for a walk, were never put off by the size of the 'stick' a man might carry, they would often look longingly at his logs and plead with their eyes that they should have it to play with, their body language screamed, 'Come on mate chuck us that stick, come on give us a go, I can do it.'

'Not blooming likely', he thought, 'get yer own.'

Some painstaking while later, the logs were enjoying their first automobile trip and being driven home in luxury to be prepared for the Yuletide ceremony.

The day had come, the fire was kindled, small sticks crackled with delight as young flames and sparks danced above, then the log itself, cut to size, slowly the log warmed to its task and turned from mottled brown to cherry red; the sun of many years that had lain dormant in the log was now released and rays of yellow orange sunshine poured into the room from the flames

As the orang-utan in him settled into his comfy chair, feet stretched out to greet the warmth, the 'burner' of the logs sighed and truly appreciated the effort of the 'fetcher' of the logs, 'good chap' he thought, 'well done', and his heart gave thanks to the great log of the salt marsh.

Do we stand on the Earth, or does the Earth hold us up?

Up the creek in a rubber boat, and with only one paddle.

It would have been about 1975; one winter evening two young men spoke of a summer adventure while supping their beer in the warm comfort of a small town pub. Cousin Roger said, 'I've always fancied travelling a river from source to the sea'.

'What a great idea,' said I.

Roger continued, 'of course it would have to be a good river, say, something like the Wye or the Severn; you know, to make it a worthwhile trip.'

I agreed with enthusiasm, trying to recall where those rivers were, never mind what they were like. This was a real adventure in the making, something to aspire to, something to achieve. . . perhaps be the hero in life for a change.

I had very little money and certainly could not afford a boat; I spoke with my wife and it was agreed that I could buy a boat and then sell it immediately after the adventure. I found a little beauty in really good condition - then, that is when I bought it - and purchased it for £40, (I'd bought cars for less). It was a four man flat bottomed inflatable dinghy with inflatable grey tubes as sides (sponsons) and a strong wooden transom at the back for fitting the engine; it had a sectioned wooden flooring, (you might think that so should the crew be sectioned for considering the idea!), and the boat came complete with pump, huge carrying bag and its own engine ; that is, two paddles!

I tested it out with a fire brigade colleague, Eddie, who knew a little overflow side stream on the River Nene where it was possible to do a circuit, returning along the main river at some lock gates - saves carrying that heavy rubber boat. The maiden voyage went well; better than the Titanic's, anyway.

'What about maps?' Quite right, it's a good idea to know where you start and where you finish and preferably what you might find in between. Maps were far too expensive for me to buy and were vulnerable to wet conditions in those days, and the Wye, now the chosen river, is so long you needed several ordnance survey maps to cover it. Solution; borrow the maps from the library - one at a time as they had rules on lending - and with high quality tracing paper, the best that money could buy, well the sort of money we had then (thick grease proof cooking paper from the kitchen; stuff that light had a job penetrating much less the pale fine lines off the maps!) painstakingly I traced the route of the river Wye from start to finish, of course I couldn't trace the whole map, so I did just the shape of the river. I did put in important features like, bridges, post offices, pubs, oh, and where the rapids were. As the river meandered across the map the more I had to make the pieces of grease proof smaller to record the detail without having big empty sections of paper, and it kept each 'map' to a manageable size.

Did I mention rapids? Yup, several of them and some quite nasty too. See! I told you it was an adventure.

Now I have the boat, even if temporary, and the 'maps', a complete set of scraps of grease proof. What about the crew? By now Cousin Roger has had a change of heart and is doing other things with life.

I explain this to a couple of motorcycling pals of mine, again over a pint; it always seemed to invigorate any conversations somehow as the fog of alcohol kindly hid reality from view. 'I'll go with you', said Fat Phil, as we knew him, 'sounds good'. During later planning conversations with him I began to wonder about his sincerity or perhaps even his state of mind, especially when he would go off on some wild ideas about having an anchor made up at the engineering works in which he was employed (gainfully or not). Yup, that's just what we need to go with an already heavy rubber boat, a heavy metal anchor to carry with sharp bits that might end up securing the boat alright, to the bottom of the river by sinking the damn thing. Note, sharp objects and rubber boats don't go well together.

Still, Fat Phil was all I had now for crew, and I tell you that boat was heavy.

We decided on a test trip on the River Great Ouse down stream from Bedford.

Our pal, little Les, drove us to a flowing backwater section off the main river that flowed by the now (and then too) disused power station. We planned to travel a few miles to the village of Great Barford and be picked up later in the day. That was the plan.

All was going reasonably, then we hit the first obstacle - for the river Great Ouse may at one time have been navigable but had ceased to be so many years gone by; there were no lock gates at the old farm and even if there were we lacked the knowledge and the winding handle. (these being two vitally important prerequisites for anyone ever considering lock gates or at least negotiating them successfully).

We lifted the boat out of the water with some difficulty and carried it past the obstacle, which interestingly in part consisted of old eel traps - also disused. We began to launch on the other side but were disturbed by the somewhat aggressive tone of the local farmer. 'Best ignored', I thought, 'least said soonest mended'. Even though we were on the run it did not satisfy the blood lust of our local landowner - obviously from the hunting fraternity, preferring beaters to pheasants in his gun sights, he continued to verbally threaten and abuse us - must have had good blood pressure.

We were now on the water and paddling like fury to put ourselves out of stone throwing or shotgun range; Fat Phil judged we were safe and began to hurl abuse back. . . I thought, 'not a good idea that, he can walk quicker than we can paddle and we're sitting ducks, (no doubt his favourite type), stuck in the middle of the river with a heavy boat..' Even if he didn't pepper the sponsons with lead , we'd never outrun him carrying this damn boat across what are now, thanks to Phil's tirade of expletives, enemy fields.

Eventually the farmer tired of his entertainment and stomped off towards his house, possibly looking for a cat or chicken to kick on his way. We needn't have worried about him damaging the boat, as that was something we were quite capable of ourselves, we didn't need his help.

After a short period of pleasant, Sun bathed paddling, we came across a weir and by its side a completely derelict lock system. 'Come on,' says Fat Phil without hesitation, and I would surmise without any use of the grey matter, 'Let's go over'. I mean, why not, he hadn't paid money he hadn't got on a boat he couldn't keep, had he?

'No, let's investigate first', I said, for after all from the top side of a weir you don't get a good view of the bottom, you get that on the way down! We tied up and had a look; the weir was not so high with about 3 steps to it, but it was adorned here and there with bits of tree stuck there that had taken the same route Phil had fancied

' Nah!' I said, 'too risky, we'll carry her round'.

Fat Phil played the master card, the ace of trumps it was, though I suspect it covered the joker underneath, 'what's the point of having the boat if you ain't going over stuff like this?'

He'd got a point, hadn't he? There we were planning a trip on one of Britain's longest rivers, filled with rapids and were baulking at a four foot weir. Reason went out of the window and I said, 'OK, but we pick our spot and don't hang about, we paddle hard to go over the lip of the weir, so's we don't get stuck.'

He agreed, at least he said he agreed, and we went for it, paddling like hell and probably making about half a knot. We cleared the top and true didn't get stuck but the bits of tree we hadn't managed to avoid had consequences. Yes, we were sinking, we'd ripped a great gash in the bottom of the boat and the wooden floor was the only thing slowing up an early bath.

We paddled to shore with a modicum of expediency considering we were beginning to get wet, turned the boat over to reveal the long scars of a short lived battle and carried the wounded, wet and heavy boat to the road on the other side of a large field. It was sometime before we found a telephone and called a surprised little Les to pick us up. Later I made repairs to my 'on loan' boat which was now unlikely to fetch the price I had paid for it ever again.

Somehow I had a suspicion that Fat Phil was not going to make the trip, despite his pub protestations that he would. About a day before the due date for embarkation on the expedition of a life time Fat Phil dropped out.

By now I'd invested too much in the whole venture, (one that wasn't even my idea in the first place), to give up, but some planning had to change, strong as I was at that age I could not carry the boat, spare clothing, saucepan, potatoes and carrots as well as the wooden flooring. So, the flooring had to be abandoned to the shed and await our return.

You may be wondering about the potatoes and carrots, well, I was not a good cook, in fact I was no cook, but I could manage boiled vegetables in an OXO cube, that and a bit of pearl barley. My plan each evening was to light a fire from the expected plentiful supply of tinder dry firewood that I would just pick up near the bank, then peel and boil my vegetable 'stew' prior to going to sleep under my upturned boat. . . on shore of course.

I had one spare set of clothes in a plastic bag. . . there, you see, I wasn't completely senseless, but come to think of it I do not recall any sleeping bag, or indeed any sleeping comforts what so ever. . . I just couldn't carry it all on my own. All I had was what I've said, that and a strong body backed up with an abundant wealth of ignorance.

How to travel to the River Wye, some 200 miles or more from home which for the uninitiated rises somewhere in the Welsh mountains and ends up in the Bristol Channel?

No problem, my Leading Fireman, a proper hero himself called Bill Scott, knew a local lorry firm that had a depot in Cardiff. Ok, so not too close to the start but at least in Wales.

I spent the day organising the contents of this giant 'kit bag' that the boat came in and made my way to the lorry park . . . don't ask how as we had no car those days. . . I can't remember. It was now night time as it was an overnight delivery to Cardiff, though the driver stopped somewhere near Oxford to grab a bite to eat. . . I don't recall what I had, perhaps a sandwich made by my wife, it certainly wouldn't have been bought as money was scarce as I have already intimated. Dawn came and Cardiff arrived; I even helped the lorry driver unload his truck. . . I had plenty of time as the lorry which would carry me north into the required mountain range wasn't leaving till later that morning.

My tired boat and even more tired body were now travelling north to the source of the Wye; a sudden, impulsive impatience had the better of me when I spotted a sign 'Haye on Wye', and just by a bridge crossing the said river I turned to the driver and said, 'this'll do me fine here'.

'Are you sure?' he asked. 'Yes, yes', I said quickly before he put anymore miles on the clock. He pulled the lorry to a halt and we unloaded the boat. I carried it to a stony shallow bank upstream of a bridge and alongside a wide and shallow river. . . not had much rain lately, which was to make life interesting later, well, actually sooner than later.

I assembled the boat and pumped up the sponsons with the foot pump as a light rain began to fall. Did I put on my waterproofs did I hear you ask? Perhaps I would, if I'd had any. The boat was ready. . . even if I wasn't. . . and onto the water it went. My first discovery, and what unfortunate timing to make it, was that when a flat bottomed boat is paddled by one man it actually goes around in a circle, my second discovery was that without the wooden rigid flooring my knees made part of the flexible rubber flooring sag deep in the water. . . I know this because underwater rocks unpleasantly and regularly hit my knees as I went over shallows. I tried two versions of knee trauma avoidance; method one was to splay my body out a bit like a cat does when you try and put it in a box. . . and it doesn't like the idea, a bit like a giant press up with hands and feet on the inflated sponsons, and just let the boat find its own route and merry way across the shallows; method two was a much simpler affair, but involved getting wet. . . I just clambered out and splashed through the shallows while hanging on to the sponson. What with the wading and the rain, the start of the still sleepless adventure was getting off to a somewhat damp start; not just body damp but spirit damp too. After what might have been a mile or so, I came to an 'interesting' bit. I've told you how easy it wasn't to man the boat, well let me describe a bit of river I came to. . . you make up your mind then.

There she is, a wide and long sweeping right handed bend, gently sloping up on the right bank with the multitude of previously flood deposited river stones, on the left a bank guarded by closed rank trees, many of them looked like they had thorns too, both roots and branches lunged outwards in a tangled and frenzied tentacle like manner, while even more frenzied white water tore at the bank, undercutting it and occasionally giving a glimpse of deep, dark and malevolent black water. It occurred to me then, and I wouldn't disagree now, that it might be safer to stay on the shallow and slower moving side of the river, and to make sure the current didn't abduct me and my boat half way round I would disembark into the shallows and walk round the bend towing the boat. As you will no doubt have already formed an opinion on the matter it was not long before I was round the bend.

An hour or so later and I and my boat sweep majestically along a very pleasant part of the river; swathes of anchored water plants rippled long under the clear water; so clear as to be deceptive of depth no doubt, a superbly rural setting, idyllic nature; a huge fish broke the surface, though I saw it not I guessed it must be a salmon. . . in any event I did not trail my fingers in the water after that. . . just in case. In fact any thought of going in water that deep was out of the question, and for a man who had no lifejacket and whose swimming ability was measured in a few feet and with the sound of his instructor giving advice while holding a long pole out ready to save him .... I reckon I can hear the Coroner's verdict of, 'questionable sanity and misadventure.'

I'd been on the water some few hours by now and partly because I'd not eaten anything for a while, and partly due to not having slept for some thirty hours or more, and perhaps partly due to being cold and wet, but mostly as I was totally disillusioned about the prospects of success never mind any enjoyment. . . I decided I'd had enough. Perhaps if I were not alone my companion would have encouraged me as I would them, but the inner me was now in full in agreement with the outer me at this stage of the game.

'Right, let's get off this damn river', said the new we, 'but where on earth do we find a suitable landing place on this watery escalator to the sea?' The two me's scoured the now steep banks as trees and fields of potentially man eating Welsh cows seemed to whiz by at an alarming rate. . . then, sheer joy, up ahead, a bridge crossing the river. 'Aha, bridge! Bridge means road; road means people; people mean transport; transport means home', we both thought. The bridge approached quickly and all hands were called on deck, powerful arms forced the paddle through the water and even more powerful water took us away. The brain screamed, 'panic!' and shouted orders to the body, 'get that blooming paddle moving you dozy thing you', or words similar but in ancient Saxon; and the river gurgled a laugh and took us under the bridge. The flat bottomed boat propelled by one man with one paddle did what it did best under the circumstances, one - it floated, two - it went round in circles. . . and the river went straight on, inexorably seawards. Seeing the last chance for a relatively straightforward landing disappearing the body injected a good shot of adrenalin and endorphins; it did the trick and soon one desperate but relieved would be adventurer stood again on blessed terra firma.

Deflating the sponsons while changing into dry clothes and with decision made to go home the matter was dealt with as urgent; with all air out of the sponsons the rubber boat was rolled up around the transom, wet clothes thrown into the dry clothes bag, now weighing considerably more than earlier, everything possible was stuffed into the giant canvas 'kit' bag. I could hardly carry it before, now suffering probably from mild hypothermia, sleep deprivation and hypo gloxaemia, the bag weighed more than ever. I think I even took the potatoes home. . . waste not want not eh? And there was still a good vegetable stew left in them.

Somehow I lifted the bag across my shoulders and began the climb from river bank to bridge road. Once up there I elected (not sure which one of me made this choice) to cross the bridge and turn left, following the course of the river. It was a long lonely walk down that very quiet road, no traffic at all. Well, there was traffic, but it was on the parallel road on the other side of the river. I eventually came to a small building with a sign on it and situated next to another bridge. Now a dawn of understanding arose in my consciousness, the sign said simply, 'Toll Road', makes sense doesn't it, why would anyone in their right mind use a toll road when there was a free one on the other side of the river? No need to answer that question. . . it had not amused me at the time. . . and to this day I cannot see the funny side of it. You try lifting that bag, let alone carry it a mile or so.

Well, enough of wallowing in self pity and a little misplaced indignation, I crossed the new found bridge and set up to thumb a lift home from wherever it is I was. Use the maps, you ask? Stuff the useless maps, there were no place names and no information much beyond the river bank which looked much the same for the next hundred miles. Good idea maps, but I urge you not to rely on cheap grease proof versions that you made yourself!

Who would give a scruffy six footer with a bag big enough to have a body in it? Not many I suspect, but one chap stopped and by luck was going somewhere in the direction of home. But wait a minute; he's driving in the wrong direction! I came from the South that morning and now I'm being kidnapped in a Northerly direction. I raised my concern over direction and I recall him saying he always went back via some place near Birmingham. . . which I'd never heard of either. . . still, the van was warm and dry, unlikely to hit any rapids and had its own engine so I kept quiet and trusted.

In all truth I cannot remember how far he drove me, nor if I had further lifts, nor by what route I went but what I can tell you is that before midnight of the day I set off on the Wye I was back home and in bed. . . knackered, and with a boat to sell.

We are the mapmakers of our own life.

'I be Thomas,' he said, 'and so very far from home'

'I be Thomas, sir. I be Cornishman Thomas Edwin Baker of Morwenstow, and in truth I do know I'll not be seeing home nor kin again. If you have but a little time to share I'd tell you of my tale. . .

'I be only 23, sir, and the winter cold has numbed my hunger gnawed bones in this God forsaken place, and the light, sir, begins to fade as I lie here in these once proud rags. Pray, stay a while, before the light dims altogether. . .

'I am the youngest living of eleven born to my dear mother Grace, sir, and we all lived at Cory, a 15th century farm of some 64 acres, an easy mile or so from the church and close by the Cornish north west coast. Even they farmers be poor these days, sir - the county is in decline and my good father Richard Baker, he needs must also work as clerk to the parish - I reckon since before I was born. I be the second Thomas in the family sir, my late brother Thomas died in Exeter age seventeen, two years afore I be born. We'm named after our grandfather sir, so we be.

'I be used to life and death, sir, being brought up on a farm and all that, and many a ship wreck would leave her dead on the shore below. The worst I recall was when I was eleven years of age - seven corpses carried from the beach to lay by the lych gate. Many of the parish turned out to help - a grand ship, the *Caledonia* of Arbroath, she came aground and was lost at Sharpnose Point in a terrible September nor' easterly gale. . . they be cliffs there sir, 300 feet sheer down to merciless ragged rocks and that wild Atlantic. The tide and longshore drift would carry the bodies north along the coast to

where the living could just find a way down to meet the dead. Swollen, drowned and rock-battered by surf they be as they lay silent awaiting burial at St Morwenna's by our vicar; a strange man indeed he was, so my father tells me, the Reverend Hawker was his name and strange indeed - but he be good of heart enough to give Christian burial to they strangers, sir. Ar he did be strange though sir, why, he smoked the Opium and spent his days staring out to sea.

The gravedigger earned his shilling that day for sure.

They be a hardy lot at Morwenstow, sir, some say wreckers and smugglers all, but not all sir, not all. Mind you, sir, if you can keep a secret, twas said that a floor at Cory once collapsed to reveal a cavern down below; no doubt for some past use that few dare speak of. . . Those years were hard, sir, except for the sea giving bounty from soul-lost ships wrecked nearby, and there were a few. Many a cottage or barn has a ship's timber at its heart. I remember well as a child two or three ships going down; and that be only they close to home, there were plenty more. . . A deadly coast for sailors sir.

The county towns were filthy places sir, and disease no stranger to their folk. Why, sewage lay in the streets sir, and mostly people starving - the 'hungry forties' I heard it called, and that they were sir. Why, later on, when the regiment was posted in Cork, we saw the ravaging toll of hunger follow a potato disease that killed the harvest year on year, the Irish died in their thousands sir, 'twas terrible indeed. They that could, emigrated, like so many did the Cornish, in their droves sir, only the new world offered any chance of life.

By the time I was seventeen sir, I had become a tailor, just like my older brother Henry, it was a poor way to turn a penny sir, but a necessity of the day. Disease had struck the county sir, and west Cornwall in the grip of cholera. By the time I was eighteen smallpox was rife and the misery seemed endless. What chance does a young man have, to find a home, a sweetheart, a wife, and work. It all seemed so hopeless.

Then, one day, I be on an errand towards the moors when some fine men came across my path. Well fed they be and tall and strong sir, all dressed in bright red uniforms.

'You lad, yes you!' shouts the recruiting sergeant at me. 'Come join us in service to her majesty Queen Victoria, come join us in adventure'. To the beat of their drum sir I did step forward. It was the 18th of May 1850 sir, they gave me a number - 3993 it be sir - and a promise of a living as I signed my name where the sergeant pointed. Oh, how I recall my heart racing as I hurried back home to Cory to tell my father that his youngest son was a tailor no more but an honourable soldier in the Queen's favourites, the Scots Fusilier Guards.

My dear mother was afraid for me and afeared to lose her youngest son, but I do believe my father was proud of me and could see that I may find a better life this way.

Are you still there sir? I cannot see much any more. It must be getting dark and the orderlies not yet lit the lamps.

I was at Alma sir, aye and at Inkerman too, such bloody fighting; the smell of gunpowder, blood and fear. Twas fearsome desperate fighting sir. At Inkerman we were outnumbered, though we didn't know it in the fog; fog so thick we didn't know who was friend nor foe till we saw their faces and bayonets. Murderous times sir - I can hear the screams now.

'Twas September last we set siege to Sebastopol, four miserable winter months ago, a November storm sank our ships that carried the where withall to see us through, and now us have precious little to comfort. Did you know sir, they made me sergeant, and I be only a young man too. Not that you can see the stripes on my rags of uniform now. . . oh so different just one year ago when we marched past Buckingham palace and our gracious Queen Victoria. We marched tall and proud: Oh! how bright the colours in the late winter sun! The heavy rhythmic crump of black boots on gravel, flags a flying, officers a shouting, the band, the crowd, 'Our Queen!' We felt on top of the world sir - invincible we were. Oh, how so much has changed. . . many a good friend has gone before me: George Ramsey, blacksmith, died just a few days ago. . . same as I have got I reckons, and good ol' Daniel Brown, another tailor like I he was sir, he was killed first day at Inkerman along with some hundred and seventy other good souls. We lost the same at Alma sir. . . tis a bloody business this war with the Russians but our worst enemy by far is nature herself. All we are sir, are grocers, weavers, tailors, labourers and carpenters, brought to a foreign land as soldiers to die in disease hunger and cold.

Tis the men killed by Russian shot or bayonet that be the lucky ones. Theirs is pain no more, yet history will mark their sacrifice with honour. What of us sir? Who merely died a death we could have had at home sir, as many a good Cornishman has. Are we not all comrades in arms sir? Are we not all children of our country? Are you still there sir? I fear I fall to a weary deep sleep. I would my dear mother was near. Please remember me sir. . . I be Thomas Edwin Baker and so very far from home. . . Du re bo genen ni oll. . .'

So spoke Thomas Baker one warm spring day as I moved grass cuttings from his memorial in the graveyard at Morwenstow.
Perhaps, should you stand and listen, he'll 'speak' to you too.
For one, I'll not forget him.

In the above story all the facts are as history shows, by poetic licence his words are mine.

Ships lost on Morwenstow rocks.
Caledonia	1842
Phoenix	1843
Eliza	1846

Thomas Edwin Baker was baptised 29th October 1831
Enlisted in Scots Fusilier Guards on 18th May 1850 and died 10th January 1855

The old farm house at Cory burned to the ground in the late 1800s.
Richard Baker buried 13.3.1860 residing at Gooseham age 73.
Grace Baker buried 8.3.1863 residing at Cory
Reverend Robert Stephen Hawker was vicar at Morwenstow from 1834 for 41 years.
In 1854 the Scots Fusilier Guards sailed from Cork to start their journey to the Black Sea.
23rd February 1854 they paraded at Buckingham Palace in front of Queen Victoria.
They landed in the Crimea in September 1854 after first being deployed in Malta, Bulgaria and Turkey.
Thomas was entitled to the Crimea medal with clasps for Alma, Inkerman and Sebastopol. A medal he would never see.
14th November 1854 a great storm sank the British ships carrying winter provisions.
At Alma on 20th September 1854 the Scots Fusilier Guards lost 11 officers and 149 men; at Inkerman 5th November 1854 they lost 9 officers and 168 men (half their strength)
George and Daniel were indeed soldiers with Thomas.
Summer in the Crimea can be 30 degrees C. Winter can drop below freezing.
1849 cholera struck west Cornwall.
1849 - 1850 smallpox epidemic.
Where is Thomas buried? Some unknown grave in the East that is forever England; he likely died of disease; cholera was a big problem and can at times kill in only a few hours. If he had been transferred to the converted barracks at Scutari in Istanbul, Turkey it would have been recorded and it isn't. Scutari was where Florence Nightingale did her pioneering work. . . which sadly was often ignored by the powers of the day. 6,000 died of cholera at Scutari.
'Du re bo genen ni oll' Cornish for 'May God be with us all'

'Do not look where you fell, but where you slipped.'

Is there a Narnia Beyond the Old Inn Door?

The lights were lamp light dim, and, under a low beamed ceiling, low windows looked out across the quayside to a river that once took sailing ships away in search of riches and adventure and into the teeth of south westerly Atlantic gales.

Inscriptions in the Churchyard bore testament to the service at sea of the town's past young men.

Just as then, the masts of boats setting out on a high tide could be seen gliding by, almost ghostly, silhouetted against a grey July evening sky.

The singer's voice was powerful, clear and full, far beyond just sound - a magic guide that knew the way and that could transport the souls in the old Inn to the dream land far away from the real and conventional world.

I sat alone, and sitting in a wooden, cold fire-place chair, I watched and listened and wondered, why I felt the way I did.

In such a place, crowded and so full of people talking, laughing, eating and drinking, they were oblivious to my inner feelings; power - not just in the physical present but in the blinding power of hindsight; longing - for what might have been had I but the courage; love - destined in parts to be unspent, those I would gladly have died for, never knowing, the secret locked in the soul till death; spirit - something that unites mind and body to a greatness, all feelings that washed like great ocean waves around my body.

The jingle jangle of guitars; voices; were they singing for others or for their own lives and dreams? 'Ah, but I might as well try and catch the wind'.

The senses brim full with dreams to be fulfilled, of those I knew and those I loved, yet knowing they were but only dreams, they were never mine nor will be, my heart 'walks along the sand and takes her hand', but I never will, for the 'rain has hung the leaves with tears', 'I want her near', 'to kill my fears', and 'everywhere I look her eyes I'd see' ; - 'Ah but I might as well try and catch the wind.'

One Guinness followed joyously in the footsteps of another to join me and be with my tapping feet and hands, but my heart drifted away to thirty or forty years ago.

I was lost in this dream world which somehow makes us different, in a different time and place. Lost in this world you can be brave, noble, wise, fulfilled - all you wish for. In this world you make no earthly mistakes - you just can't.

I felt my youth, my strength, my old motorbike was parked outside, and my leather jacket on the back of the chair - and then the song was over.

Lost in this dream as we sit there, we could be someone else, a sailor, a miner, or labourer enjoying the fatigue of honest toil, simple but also simply heroic, and in another time too, of centuries ago.

Feelings are immortal, they are eternally the same, had Scots Fusilier Thomas Baker of Morwenstow been here before he sailed from Devon to die a thousand miles from home he may well have felt just as me as he listened to songs of the sea. Here, then, is an immortal link between our children, us and our ancestors.

Sitting alone but self contained, not afraid, filled with the optimistic power of youth; it's as though a spirit enters and takes you to a magic place, words cannot describe - you must go and see for yourself. A sense of power flows through you that could easily lure you and tempt you to do crazy and impossible things that you will, in the moment, believe possible.

The blood of your ancestors flows through your veins and listens to the music with you, whether the joy of song lifting the hearts of miners in the dark or the beat of drums on the cold Crimean winter 'heights of Sebastopol'. If I were with them, I would feel the same as them, and also they with us, for feelings live forever.

That's what it is. . . Now I understand.

Catch the Wind lyrics by Donovan

How foolish to seek in the outside world
that which resides within.
Zen

Just an old man watching pigeons.

We rarely see it all; we often make a judgement on the little we do see.

Some twelve years ago now I lived in a 1960s bungalow in a small town in Cambridgeshire, one of six in the close. At one end, and closed to traffic, was a large patch of grass and a few aging ornamental blossom trees. A footpath ran along its edge and I would on occasion go that way for the riverside walk in to town. Just around the corner lived a kindly old Polish gentleman who kept and bred racing pigeons ... I know this, as the blooming things would circle over my washing and car before deciding where to go next.

One day I noticed a thin scruffily dressed man in a dirty grey long coat loitering seemingly purposefully under the trees; he wore an old cap and had glasses that showed he had a damaged right eye, possibly blinded. I wondered what could possibly be the attraction under these trees for one, who to all intents and purposes, looked like a penniless and unkempt vagrant.

As I walked by, I merely acknowledged him with a look and a nod and continued into town. To my surprise he was still there when I returned. I thought, 'poor old chap, I'll speak with him this time.' I'm glad I did, and this is what he told me. . . 'I'm waiting to see the pigeons come home; I used to keep them myself once, he has some champion birds you know.' I didn't speak much but nodded my encouragement that I was interested in his story, for he spoke simply but very well, obviously being once an accomplished man. 'I was in the war, you know, (2nd World War 1939-45) I was one of Montgomery's body guards.' I began to think he might be spinning a yarn of fantasy but continued to acknowledge him. 'All my pals are dead now, I'm the only one left alive. . . We met the Russians you know, our two armies came together. . . It could have been very dangerous; no one knew what would happen. As we approached I shouted out in Russian,'Ladna, ladna, engliski soldat', so as they would not fire on us.' I knew that what he'd said was 'it's Ok its ok ... we're English soldiers', as I had a smattering of basic Russian myself. Now I'm beginning to believe him more. 'After the war I was invited to Moscow by the friends I'd made when we met on the front line, they took me to Red Square and Lenin's tomb, we didn't have to queue, we were taken straight to the front, they treated me very well, like a hero in fact. Now all my pals are dead and gone, I have no one, no family either. Do you know I once owned the old cinema in town, where that big supermarket is now; I sold it for a good price too. . . Ah, look, here come a couple of his pigeons, excuse me please, I'll just make a note.'

He made his note, we shook hands and I left him with his long vigil; I had stopped off to say hello to a tramp and I walked away saying goodbye to a forgotten hero in tramps clothing; a hero with no one to tell his tale . I walked away with a lesson in life and respect for that lonely little old man; I walked away with memories. . . Except I don't even know his name; I never saw him again.

There's an inside and an outside to all. Everyone has their story.

When you are sorrowful, look again in your heart,
and you shall see that in truth you are weeping for that which has
been your delight
Kahlil Gibran

Miscellaneous

That little bump on the head

It was just one of those annoying little things, one of those little bumps under the skin, sebaceous cysts he thought they called them, and, as baldness wended its merry way, that little bump became more prominent - almost a feature of the landscape as it were.

Well, he popped along to the nearby village surgery and asked them what they thought.

'Ah, you've come to the right place; we can fix that for you here, no problem. We can carry out minor surgical operations right here in the village practice. Come on, let's make you an appointment.'

Now you can't ask much better than that, can you?

The due day duly arrived and he attended early as was his habit. They led him into a long room, which still seemed to be partly shared by the public, and sat him on an old wooden dining chair.

'Would you mind if our new practice doctor did your little operation?' smiled the practice nurse, luring him into a false sense of security. (Translation; We've got a total ham fisted novice learner just joined us, who's never even seen a cyst never mind operated on one and we reckon you'll make a fine expendable guinea pig for him to experiment on.)

Not being able to translate medical speak at the time our unsuspecting friend offered himself for sacrifice, 'No problem, go ahead, do your worst.' And sitting there comfortingly reminded himself of who and what he was, brave and noble fire-fighter, man who'd walked the wild moors and slept in the odd bus shelter, one time pot-holer and long time martial artist; surely he could handle this little task with no fear.

First came a quiet and calm introduction by the doctor, followed by the pain killing injection, well, not all of it, some small amount may have gone through the needle before our novice surgeon managed to persuade the two halves of the syringe to part company from each other; the resultant release of anaesthetic sprayed over the victim's, er, patient's face and half anaesthetised the surgery contents. The doctor fumbled and apologised.

Still, not to worry, eh?

The practice nurse looked on. . . as much there to comfort the doctor as the patient.

Now came the good bit - the bit where the doctor picked up the razor edged scalpel. Remember, the bump is high on the forehead and can't be seen by its owner without a mirror, and they weren't going to give him one of them! He just had to trust in the competence of this fine and highly trained young medical professional.

Still acting out the, 'give it yer best shot' macho man, he mentally prepared for the next move. It was a bit of a surprise really, because he felt nothing.

However, he heard and saw everything; he heard the young doctor in an agitated and profusely apologetic voice repeatedly intersperse his name with 'sorry'. . . 'oh dear, I'm so sorry' …   And he saw the practice nurse burst into emergency mode racing down the surgery and returning quickly with some wad of absorbent which she pressed on his forehead, 'This should soak some of the blood up' she said, no doubt with an unseen exasperated glare at the doctor.

Well, with little bump removed and a few more than necessary stitches in a gash that should only have been a hole he was fine to leave.

'Thank you,' he said as he left.

'Sorry,' they said as he went.

New evidence:
Is this the truth about the
Billy Goats Gruff Family?

This story is based on the Norwegian Folk Tale of three brother goats, the Gruff brothers, who sought pastures green on the other side of the river. The only bridge was controlled by a supposedly wicked Troll. The first two goats to cross were allowed to pass by unmolested, they had each betrayed their elder brother who they said would be along shortly; and true enough he was and he beat the Troll and continued to join his younger brothers. (We can only assume they kept it a secret how they managed to cross the bridge unharmed). You know, I can see some interesting latent messages in this story, especially for Trolls.

I suggest we revisit this tale and see what the truth might have been. The author recommends that those of a nervous disposition, the squeamish, vegans and goat herders find something else to read. You have been warned.

It was a fine summer's day, and the three Billy Goat Gruffs were out doing what they did best. . . eating. They didn't care that much what they ate, they'd been up trees for apples, had the bark off saplings, and even once letting a camper wake to discover his only washed and drying underwear had disappeared off the line outside his tent.

In fact, the three goats, Little-Gruff, Middle-Gruff and Big-Gruff had virtually scoffed their way through most of the west side of the river that ran through the valley.

They had many times observed the verdant lush grasses on the other side waving an inviting welcome to them in the summer breeze. . . But the river kept them from accepting.

'Let's find a way across to that lovely grub over there,' said Middle-Gruff. The other two, salivating drool down their beards, agreed at once. Big-Gruff, who was almost verging on being the sensible one, said, 'OK, we'll travel the bank upstream looking for a good crossing place. . . we'll go today . . . but we must stick together, for don't you remember our parents warning us never to cross the river. . . Remember. . . just before they disappeared?'

They three brothers in hooves sauntered the upstream bank, occasionally stopping to browse on thistle and gawp salivating at the lush field that would soon be theirs, all theirs, a place to die for, such paradise as it looked. Nary had a conscious thought crossed their minds why there were no other animals out there feasting on such plenty.

It wasn't long before Little-Gruff was well out in front, he was a 'gobby little know it all', couldn't be told a thing by his elder brothers. 'I know that', he would bleat in the face of advice, 'do you think I'm stupid', as his brothers tried to teach him something. . . and even then it wasn't much of a something either.

'Stay in sight Little-gruff', shouted Big-Gruff through a mouthful of nettles, 'do not cross the river without us!' Middle-Gruff shook his coat of the nettle flavoured spit that he'd just been sprayed with and passed wind. Big-Gruff thought he heard a reply in the breeze, 'yeah, yeah, yeah, dopey', but he wasn't too sure as the sound of salivated nettle shoots chomping around in his mouth had obliterated his hearing - except for the chomping that is.

Middle-Gruff was chomping well too and had been since waking for breakfast and yet, all the while, his mind was on the field; His field, full of his grass, and as he dreamed he dreamed a horrific image. In his mind, Little-Gruff was there first, and eating, eating his grass in his field. 'Er, Big-Gruff, I think I'd better catch up with dear Little-Gruff. . . You know . . . make sure the poor little chap is ok and doesn't cross the river to my field. . . I mean our field, without us. I'll, er, just move ahead a bit quicker, OK?' Without awaiting reply, Middle-Gruff, seething with envy and filled with fermenting nettle leaves walked on briskly, without ever looking back to his big brother.

'Good chap, well done', said Big-Gruff, spotting a succulent bed of watercress, which was now all his, and his alone. Big-Gruff sent up a silent prayer for the find to the great Capricorn, Patron Saint of goats, who some say resided in an eternal-summer land filled with everlasting harvests.

Big-Gruff sauntered, chomped and salivated; Middle-Gruff ran, seethed and passed wind; but Little-Gruff was far away and had happened across something rather interesting. . . half hidden by dense foliage. . . a bridge! More importantly it was a bridge and pathway to his field and his grass.

With eyes only on his field across the river and not a single moment of conscious thought for his brothers or his missing parent's warnings Little-Gruff was off, the bridge's wooden boards clonking to the sound of his little hooves, 'trip trap trip trap trip tra. . .'

Horror of all horrors, something from the world of a goat's worst nightnannies leapt over the railings and stood hunched and threatening in front of him. . . It was a Troll.

'Who's that crossing my bridge?' demanded the Troll, and some would say he was quite within his Troll rights to ask.

'Gulp, it's only little me, Little-Gruff', quaked the trembling Little-Gruff, babying himself in the hope of sympathy. 'Please don't eat me, I am thin and starving. . . I only want to go and eat in my field. . . I mean that field, if you let me go my bigger brother will be along soon and he is much fatter than I, you could eat him instead'. Some thoughts crossed the Troll's mind, a rare experience, but it occurred to the Troll, that firstly, that field was his, secondly he too was starving and thirdly, he hadn't eaten a goat in months. That was enough thinking for the day.

Little-Gruff looked at the grass, his grass; the Troll looked at the goat, his goat, and before Little-Gruff could move or call for help the Troll was on him; mercifully a swift death;

with the goat's limp body under his arm the Troll swung his body over the rail and under the bridge. There, up on a dry bank in the shelter of the bridge and hidden by undergrowth, the Troll sat comfortably surrounded by a scattered bone collection, a hobby of some years now, and he tucked in to the tastiest freshest goat he'd had in ages.

Only half way through his dinner he heard another customer arriving, a trifle annoyed by the disturbance at mealtime he felt he must still respond to anything crossing his bridge. His bridge, did you ask? Yes, his bridge; a Troll bridge, built by the Troll, for the Troll, it was the Troll that built it and maintained it, not the government, not the council, but old Trolley boy himself, and hard work it had been at times too. 'Trip. . . Trap. . . Trip. . . Trap' came the heavier hooves of Middle-Gruff, rushing to catch up and be with his little brother. . . he was almost across too when with great power and speed the troll vaulted the railings to confront his latest 'customer'. 'And who is this that crosses me bridge', demanded the Troll, never having been one much for grammar, as he'd left school early to take up a trade.

Middle-Gruff was made of the same stuff as his younger brother, only his stuff was older and bigger. 'Ah, mister Troll Sir, tis only I, Middle-Gruff. . . if you'd just let me pass by sir I can promise you a much bigger goat is coming this way as we speak'.

Middle-Gruff was sure that the Troll's eyes looked away for a moment as if to see if a bigger goat was indeed close by, it was his chance to make a run for it back to his now beloved Big-Gruff brother. Too late and too slow, Middle-Gruff's first twitch was his last twitch and soon he joined his younger brother under the bridge. The Troll finished his first course and without a break, nor drink of water, and with only a belch between them, went straight on with the second course. The Troll hadn't eaten so well in years, 'Lovely grub', he thought, using a fine rib bone to pick bits of meat from between his teeth, 'mmm lovely grub'.

Above him the Troll heard a heavy clatter on his wooden

boards, 'TRIP TRAP TRIP TRAP'. What a busy day it had been, what with all the exertion, dealing with two awkward customers and being stuffed by that huge dinner he was drowsy and could hardly move any way. The Troll settled back with hands on belly and afternoon napped.

Above the Bridge, above the Troll, and above the dismembered bodies of his brothers, mum and dad and several other relatives, Big-Gruff was blissfully unaware. Trip trapping his heavy hooves across the wood enjoying the sound it made and bathed in glorious late afternoon sunshine he eyed the lush grass in his new field. Big-Gruff looked around for his brothers but couldn't see them, sure that they had found the bridge and crossed over, he assumed that they had been at a good dinner and were now resting somewhere out of sight. 'I'll eat first', Big-Gruff said to himself, an old habit, 'then I'll join my brothers later'. Big-Gruff stuffed himself silly with the sweetest, lushest grass he'd ever encountered, until he could hardly move. 'Lovely grub', he thought trying to tongue an awkward bit of leaf from between his teeth, 'mmm, lovely grub'. As evening approached and night's dusk put out the lights Big-Gruff settled down comfortably in some long grasses that sheltered him from the night breezes of the valley.

'What a good day', thought Big-Gruff, 'what a good day', then just as he closed his eyes to sleep he thought he heard something move nearby. . . and. . . as night fell upon him. . . so did the Troll.

'What a good day', thought the Troll, 'what a good day', as Big-Gruff's lifeless body was dragged off to join his brothers.

Well, there we have it, one version of The three Billy Goats Gruff; food for thought eh? You didn't have to read it. . . and you can always write your own.

In the original, the two younger goats, so quick to betray their siblings, were let go across by the Troll. . . trusting old Troll eh? Then that vicious bad tempered big Billy goat Gruff turns up and in an unprovoked frenzy murders the Troll, who is only asking the question, 'who's that crossing my bridge?' It was murder right enough but Big Billy Goat Gruff could have got off with troll-slaughter due to diminished common sense and only done twenty hours community service no doubt.

The murdered Troll would have left behind a number of grieving dependants who had to move out of the area because Big Billy Goat Gruff was still free. It would not be long before the bridge fell in to disrepair for want of maintenance and the council would refuse to do it as it had never been adopted. The valley would thereafter always be divided. Nothing would be reported in the papers and no memorial to the Troll ever erected. The courts, headed by Sir Hugh Wilberforce Gruff would make sure of that.

'Change the way you look at things,
and the things you look at will change.'

A Winter's Night on Irsha Street.

Comfortingly back home in my contemporary kitchen, doors locked tight and electric lights all on. . . I sit with my elbows resting on my old pine table, its enduring strength a prop to my insecurities. My much loved table, despite its many sufferings, it has stood the test of time. I feel the warmth from the log fire sending out its comforting glow across the room, the burning wood crackling a song of the forest, accompanied by a hushed but harmonious howling as air is drawn through small iron vents at its base. Both the table and fire somehow seem to connect me to the past, with happy memories of days that were perhaps not as durable. I pick up and open a note book and begin to write for you, though my senses are still somewhat bewildered by the events that infused a visit I made earlier that evening to a little place called Irsha Street.

Irsha, almost a place that time has forgotten, was a quaint little street in a remote old fishing village. Irsha is long and narrow, with only a car width road and no pavements; many small alley ways disappear left and right into a darkness that has lived for centuries between the houses, some paths disappear inland towards the hill and some out towards the sea.

The houses on one side of Irsha stand elevated from the sea on a cliff like old stone sea wall. Lower down, even closer to the sea, once stood other old seafarer's houses, but these had failed to endure tide and time and stand no more; no trace remains, as if they never were.

As I write this, something is telling me that I am not entirely alone in this seemingly empty kitchen, something gently touches the crown of my head as if to say they know what I am doing. . . perhaps a warning, but there is no sense of dread, not this time, just a presence that has joined me from where I know not and for why I know not.

In any event, alone or accompanied, I'll still share with you of my visit.

'Call in for a cup of tea sometime', Joe'd said.

So, on this wet winter's night, as occasional drizzle drifted here and there dropping gentle rain on the nearby rugged Devon coast, I thought it time I accepted his kind offer.

I left my car in the poorly lit and deserted quayside car park, put on my long black overcoat and adjusted my scarf and woolly hat against the damp. As I walked alongside the waterfront railings into the darkness towards Irsha, pinpoints of coloured light brightened the far murk across the bay; warnings to sailors of sandbars and rocks; sparkling beacons distant in a dark foreboding sea. As I entered Irsha Street the wind dropped and all became hushed, even my shoes on the tarmac were strangely silent, as were the many houses I passed on either side. The street itself was deserted and seemingly so were most of the houses, only one or two showed a light, and even then no one was to be seen through the glass, I didn't like to peer inside for fear of someone looking out only to be disturbed by such ill mannered intrusion. Directions and landmarks I'd been given soon led me to the house I sought; it was pleasantly easy to find in fact.

It was dark in Irsha except for the few dim street lights that sporadically lit the narrow roadway; a roadway wet from earlier rain that evening. There was a light on in the house and I could clearly see through the window I had found the right place; my host was sitting in a large chair in the far left corner of what appeared surprisingly to be quite a large room. I soon found the door, and knocked.

I didn't have to wait long before the door opened and a smiling face greeted me.

'Come on in', Joe said, 'come on through'.

I bowed my head through the low doorway and entered.

Once inside, I found the house was much larger than I had anticipated, I previously thought that they were all small two up two down cottages along Irsha. As is so often the case, what we think we see isn't what we think it is; there's many a surprise in life for us all about what we thought we saw. The entrance lobby and first room through which we walked was unlit except for light coming through an opening to the next room, but I could still see the beamed ceiling, tasteful furniture and pictures; underfoot I felt the cold and uneven flags of the 16thC stone floor. We moved through the opening into a similarly presented room. My host, a worldly wise, stocky and affable man of some years was talking to someone that I could not see; it all became clear as he ushered me through a low opening to yet more rooms at the back of the house and there was the lady of the house, the object of his conversation, quietly making tea. She was a pleasant talkative lady who invited me to remove my coat and sit a while and 'did I want sugar in my tea'.

'That's a relief', I thought, at least he's not talking to imaginary people; or worse still, something else of which my mind would rather stay in ignorance.

It was a large and interesting back room, with a central inglenook fireplace complete with old ironmongery for hanging meat and cooking pots; all around were misshapen ancient walls, on which paintings of many seascapes and sailing ships hung as testimony to a maritime past, and floors that leaned this way and that in no particular order. As my tea slowly went cold in my hands my host's conversation continued absorbingly, with tales of smugglers, murders, secret tunnels and of footsteps heard crossing the wooden floors of the empty rooms above. Joe spoke quietly of these things in the manner of a man that knew the truth of this world.

Both the building and its contents smacked of another age; it was almost as though I had gone back in time, as though the energy left by the past was still present. The conversation led me to sense that I too might 'see', 'hear' or 'feel' the past. After tea I was shown around the labyrinth of rooms and stairs of all shapes in which many a hiding place could remain a secret for all times. I stood on steps where once stood the murdered and I walked the floor over which many a contraband barrel had rolled, I looked to the walls and floors beyond which lay secret places and hidden history, in part I felt that my soul saw more than my eyes.

How often have we glimpsed something from the corner of our eye but when we look again there is nothing there ... or was there? The child that plays with imaginary friends, or sees something in the night, is soon put right by the knowing and fearful adult. . . 'best not to look. . . no, no, don't look. . . don't tell me any more. . . there's nothing there. . . Go to sleep, close your eyes.'

Whose eyes is it that were really closed?

Another cup of tea and the invisible hours had passed us by as though they never were. . .

I picked up my nearly drunk tea. . . the cup was cold to my touch. . . 'Gosh, is that the time?' I said, glancing at the digital watch on my wrist, 'I really must be away home and leave you in peace; thank you so much for your timeless hospitality, most interesting'. . . and, reflecting upon their historical revelations, thinking privately, 'and almost beyond belief too'.

I bid farewell and re-crossed the 16th Century stones to the door with Joe, the gentleman of the house; he too seemed timeless, as though he were part of the fabric of the old Inn himself, at one with the hostelry, attuned to the heartbeat of the house that held so many secrets.

Buttoning my long dark overcoat it seemed to fit me better than when I'd arrived, I somehow felt taller, more comfortable and strong, as though younger now, almost like being someone else; I stepped into the rain damped narrow street, the old Inn door closing quietly behind me.

I began a silent, contemplative walk eastwards along the hushed and still deserted Irsha; my mind wandered to the events of the evening, then I glimpsed something from the corner of my eye; something large that loomed out of the darkness. My eyes slowly accustomed to the night and a faint breeze carried the smell of salt air to my nostrils and the creaking of timbers and rigging to my ears. . . as the darkness was eased apart by shifting clouds a faint moonlight revealed an ancient ship of two masts riding newly at anchor in the deep water channel, rolling so gently in harmony with the tireless estuary waves, her sails furled. . . I thought I saw movement on deck, thought I saw the swing of the hurricane lamp. . . and then nature drew its curtain of clouds once more to hide the moon and I was left with a darkness within a darkness and the sound of water lapping the rocks. A previously unknown knowing came in to my head, she was a Brigantine, yes, that's what she was, a Brigantine, two masted and shallow draft. . . and not long home from sea too.

If she was truly there or not, now I cannot say, but that night I knew exactly where she was, how tall, how rigged and all such detail that could be seen and told.

All was made more real by the clearly audible, slow soporific swoosh of gentle waves lapping the shore in slow rhythm, with the pauses between almost as though the sea were holding its breath.

As I passed by the little slipway I sensed three men, short and stocky, wearing mufflers and caps, heaving a laden row boat further up the stone slip, for the tide was still not yet passed to the ebb. I did not linger to watch, but somehow intuition told me what they were doing; contraband; how thankful I was now that I had left when I did, this was no place for the faint hearted and those men would not be best pleased to be discovered.

The spectre of a long gone past began to haunt Irsha, and I edged nearer the middle of the empty street for safety. I walked on quietly not wishing to disturb what was happening, yet slightly fearful and knowing I could no longer turn back, it was as if I had entered the sorcerer's cave and now fear to wake him.

Irsha is long and narrow but this night it seemed ever more so, time seemed confused in some way, the street, like time, never seeming to end. Then something walked alongside me, I became aware of two men, who though strongly built seemed of a desperately nervous disposition; their nailed boots trod not on tarmac but on rutted stones and there was a fleeting whiff of rotting vegetation and sewage in the air as if it lay in the street. They walked in a greater darkness than I. It would appear that the men did not see me, or if they did I meant nothing to them; nothing I saw seemed to see me, a cloak of timely invisibility covered me, though at times I feared it would not.

I became aware of the untidy ramshackle quay side with its frames, boxes and nets and the river beyond as though there were now no houses between me and they.

I walked on and on, passing some small houses that seemed no more than pauper's hovels and into one of which both men vanished. It was as though they never were, except that the sound of their voices lingered on, it was the last thing to pass. . . a curse it was, 'twas press gangs working the town that they cursed. . . then their voices followed them into their greater silence, and Irsha was quiet again.

Driven by an unexpected and transient gust of wind some smoke drifted across the street; the smell of wood smoke filled the air and my now heightened senses. I walked on, still slow and in a silence, sensing, as I passed by, places born of centuries past itself, the shivers, the hunger, the fear, a sense of little expectation from life but to survive, a sense of

those waiting in vain but in hope of a loved son's return from the sea.

I walked out of Irsha and onwards towards the Church and graveyard where no doubt we might find their ageing bones and if lucky some inscription marking their passing, even if they be lost at sea.

However, just like the many dead of past and distant wars the poor leave no markers, except perhaps in our hearts that may be touched by their troubled spirits even today.

Somehow transformed by my journey into Irsha words of noble poetry and stories of the soul sprang to mind and those words triggered feelings; not unlike hearing songs or stories that can fill us all with feelings, feelings as if we were still there, like when we were young; feelings that connect us to our own past and even to our own ancestors and knowing what they must have done and felt. . . For in part, we are them. In our mind we can belong to a different place and time. . . even if for a brief while; a glimpse is all we need in order to 'know'. You must have been there yourself; you must have felt this in your own being sometime, somewhere. Irsha was well behind me now and I carried only memories with me towards the live music that came from the Seagate Hotel bar, to my left a glint of Moonlight which had evaded the clouds crossed the river to the street lights of Instow.

The pub was full of friendly people enjoying the warmth of drink and music, the bar was full of life. Warm applause greeted the rag tag and bobtail group of musicians as the song ended, leaving me residual feelings. . . feelings that were trapped briefly in time past. . . Once again I felt the strength of my youth and the courage of my forebears, my mind had transcended time and distance if only for a while. I ordered a Guinness from the bar and I reflected on an old saying, 'if the end is part of the story, then death is a part of living'. . . Perhaps we too will 'live on' somehow too. . .

In memory of my friend Joe:
a soul can be sparked to kinship that lasts a lifetime.

Joe Webb 25th June 1942 ~ 2nd November 2011

'The end of anything is never a stopping point;
It is merely the doorway to new discoveries'

Homeward, once again.

Autumn dead leaves scampered, as if alive, so, so quickly; quickly tumbling unfaltering across the sticky estuary mud; not stopping they, and, all in a rush, onwards seawards they were bent.

Despite the ebbing tide, still undaunted, little waves would come and lap the new born shoreline. The wind was strong, as it ever can be, and it came from afar, from the North, the land of the white bear; it had travelled far to chill the bones of the watcher on the quay that day. The watcher saw it all, the leaves, the changing sky of grey, the retreating waves harried by the wind; he marvelled at it all, and, seeing darkness on its way he turned his thoughts and boots to homeward, once again.

When I let go of who I am. . . I become who I might be
Lao Tzu

Beyond the Spirit Seas and Mountains the answer sleeps,
put one foot in front of the other and go and wake it up.

You may contact the author via:
www.goodshortstories.weebly.com
www.taichidevon.weebly.com

Edward Gaskell *publishers*
DEVON